Ferdinand de Saussure

Flaubert: The Uses of Uncertainty

Structuralist Poetics: Structuralism, Linguistics,
  and the Study of Literature

The Pursuit of Signs: Semiotics, Literature, Deconstruction

Barthes

On Deconstruction: Theory and
  Criticism after Structuralism

Jonathan Culler

Ferdinand de Saussure

REVISED EDITION

Cornell University Press

ITHACA, NEW YORK

Revised edition first published 1986 by Cornell University Press.

International Standard Book Number (cloth) 0-8014-1917-4
International Standard Book Number (paper) 0-8014-9389-7
Library of Congress Catalog Card Number 86-6302
Printed in the United States of America
*Librarians: Library of Congress cataloging information
appears on the last page of the book.*

The paper in this book is acid-free and meets the guidelines for permanence and durability of the Committee on Production Guidelines for Book Longevity of the Council on Library Resources.

IN MEMORIAM

VERONICA FORREST - THOMSON

1947 – 1975

Contents

Preface to the Revised Edition

For this new edition of *Ferdinand de Saussure*, I have made minor changes and corrections throughout. Significant additions come in discussion of Saussure's debt to Hippolyte Taine, in the treatment of Saussure's work on anagrams, and in the account of recent uses of Saussure in contemporary Marxism, psychoanalysis, and deconstruction. Saussure's relevance to what theorists and commentators seem determined to label the age of post-structuralism is, I believe, a question of considerable interest. I treat it primarily by describing his thought itself rather than trying to follow his influence on many thinkers of the 1970s and 1980s. I do find it striking, though, how frequently theorists draw upon Saussurian insights in order to contest what they take to be the principles of structuralism. Thus Terry Eagleton's lively and polemical *Literary Theory: An Introduction* takes as the decisive critique of structuralism a Saussurian principle, that meaning is the product of differences—in Eagleton's words, that "every sign would seem to be made up of a potentially infinite tissue of differences," a principle that he makes the basis of post-structuralism. The possibility of using Saussure, the original structuralist, in a critique of structuralism suggests, of course, that his work contains different lines of argument, whose angles and force must be calculated. Above all, it shows that reading Saussure can help one question the facile distinction between structuralism and post-structuralism, which may caricature structuralism and transfer to post-structuralism what is most interesting in structuralist writings. Reading Saussure may therefore be an excellent way of sorting out what is going on today in that strange realm called "theory."

JONATHAN CULLER

Ithaca, New York
January, 1986

Abbreviations

References to Saussure's *Course in General Linguistics* are given in the text and use the following abbreviations:

Course: Ferdinand de Saussure, *Course in General Linguistics*. Translated by Wade Baskin. New York: McGraw Hill, 1976, and London: Fontana, 1974.

Cours: Ferdinand de Saussure, *Cours de linguistique générale*. Edited by Tullio de Mauro. Paris: Payot, 1973. This is the standard edition. The pagination of the text is the same as in earlier Payot editions. These page numbers can also be used to find passages in Roy Harris's new translation of the *Course*. London: Duckworth, 1983.

Engler: Ferdinand de Saussure, *Cours de linguistique générale*. Critical edition by Rudolf Engler. Wiesbaden: Otto Harrassowitz, 1967–74. This edition prints the students' notes from which the *Course* was constructed. I cite it only when referring to those notes.

In quoting from the *Course*, I give page references to both the English and French editions. All translations are my own.

I am indebted to Kate Patterson, Wlad Godzich, and especially J. L. M. Trim for their comments on the original manuscript and to Jeff Nunokawa for help in preparing the revised edition.

Ferdinand de Saussure

Introduction

Ferdinand de Saussure is the founder of modern linguistics, the man who reorganized the systematic study of language and languages so as to make possible the achievements of twentieth-century linguistics. This alone makes him worth studying, but he has other claims to our attention as well.

First, together with his two great contemporaries, Emile Durkheim in sociology and Sigmund Freud in psychology, he helped to set the study of human behavior on a new footing. These three thinkers realized that one could not approach an adequate understanding of human practices and institutions if one treated human behavior as a series of events similar to events in the physical world. A scientist can study the behavior of objects under certain conditions, such as the trajectories of projectiles fired at different angles and velocities, or the reactions of a chemical substance to a variety of temperatures. She can describe what happens and try to explain why without paying any attention to ordinary people's impressions or ideas about these matters. But human behavior is different. When studying human behavior the investigator cannot simply dismiss as subjective impressions the meaning behavior has for members of a society. If people see an action as impolite, that is a crucial fact, a social fact. To ignore the meanings actions and objects have in a society would be to study mere physical events. Anyone analyzing human behavior is concerned not with events themselves but with events that have meaning.

Saussure, Freud, and Durkheim also saw that the study of human behavior misses its best opportunities if it tries to trace the historical causes of individual events. Instead, it must focus on the functions events have within a general social framework. It must treat social facts as part of a system of conventions and values. What are the values and conventions which enable people to live in society, to communicate with one another, and generally to behave as they do? If one tries to answer these questions, the result is a discipline very different from one which replies to questions about the historical causes of various events. Saussure and his two contemporaries established the supremacy of this type of investigation, which looks for an underlying system rather than individual causes, and they thus made possible a fuller and more apposite study of human experience.

Second, by his methodological example and various prophetic suggestions, Saussure helped to promote semiotics, the general science of signs and systems of signs, and structuralism, an important trend in contemporary anthropology and literary criticism as well as in linguistics. The revival of interest in Saussure in the past few years is largely due to the fact that he has been the inspiration for semiotics and structuralism as well as for structural linguistics.

Third, in his methodological remarks and general approach to language Saussure gives us a clear expression of what we might call the formal strategies of Modernist thought: the ways in which scientists, philosophers, artists, and writers working in the early part of this century tried to come to terms with a complex and chaotic universe. How does one cope, systematically, with the apparent chaos of the modern world? This question was being asked in a variety of fields, and the replies which Saussure gives—that you cannot hope to attain an absolute or Godlike view of things but must choose a perspective, and that within this perspective objects are defined by their relations with one another, rather than by essences of some kind—are exemplary. Saussure enables us to grasp with unusual clarity the strategies of Modernist thought.

Finally, Saussure's treatment of language focuses on problems which are central to new ways of thinking about the human subject, and especially about the intimate relation between language and mind. If "man" is indeed the "language animal," a creature whose dealings with the world are characterized by the structuring and differentiating operations that are most clearly manifested in human language, then it is Saussure who set us on his track. When we speak of the human tendency to organize things into systems by which meaning can be transmitted, we place ourselves in what is very much a Saussurian line of thought.

These contributions—to linguistics, to the social sciences generally, to semiotics and structuralism, to Modernist thought, and to our conception of human beings—make Saussure a seminal figure in modern intellectual history, and this book must range widely over linguistics, semiotics, philosophy, and the social sciences if it is to define Saussure's importance. But paradoxically, Saussure himself wrote nothing of general significance. A book on the vowel system of early Indo-European language, a doctoral thesis on the use of the genitive case in Sanskrit, and a handful of technical papers are all that he ever published. Nor did he leave behind a rich hoard of unpublished writings. His influence, both within and beyond linguistics, is based on something he never wrote. Between 1907 and 1911, as professor at the University of Geneva, he gave three courses of lectures on general linguistics. After his death, in 1913, his students and colleagues decided that his teachings should not be lost and constructed out of various sets of lecture notes a volume entitled *Cours de linguistique générale*—a course in general linguistics.

I shall have more to say about the strange genesis of the *Course*, the way in which the published text was put together. For the moment, the important point is this: whatever Saussure's general significance for modern thought—and it is considerable—he himself was first and foremost, perhaps even exclusively, a linguist, a student of language. Someone who knows Saussure only by reputation, as the founder of modern linguistics, promoter of a new conception of language, and inspiration for anthropologists and literary critics, might expect to find the *Course in General Linguistics* a book full of broad generalizations, portentous observations about the nature of language and mind, elaborate and eloquent theories about social and communicative behavior. In fact, nothing could be further from the truth. What strikes one most forcibly in the *Course* is Saussure's active and scrupulous concern for the foundations of his subject.

His concern with the nature of language and the foundations of linguistics takes the form of a questioning of the assumptions we make when we talk about language. For example, if you make a noise and at some other time I make a noise, under what conditions would we be justified in saying that we had uttered the same words? Such questions may seem trivial. One might be tempted to reject them as pointless quibbling, arguing that we simply *know* whether two people have uttered the same words or not. But the point is, how do we know? What is involved in knowing this? For whatever is involved is part of our knowledge of language, our knowledge of the units of that language. Such questions are far from trivial. If we are to analyze a language we must be able to form a clear and coherent idea of the units or elements of that language. If, for example, we are to think of the "word" as a unit of language, then we must know how we determine that two people have uttered the same word, though the actual physical sounds they made were different.

Saussure asks fundamental and probing questions that linguists before him had failed to ask, and he provides answers that have revolutionized the way language is studied. Though the solutions and definitions he offers might initially seem of interest only to students of linguistics, they have direct bearing on the fundamental problems of what the French call the "human sciences": the disciplines that deal with the world of meaningful objects and actions (as opposed to physical objects and events themselves). Saussure's reflections on the sign and on sign-systems pave the way for a general study of the ways in which human experience is organized.

This wider significance is doubtless of greater interest to readers of this book than debates about the precise nature of Saussure's distinctions and linguistic categories, and therefore discussion in the following chapters will always aim toward larger issues. But if we are to grasp the radical implications of Saussure's ideas we must follow the logic of his argument in some detail. We must go back, with Saussure, to first principles and ask elementary questions about human language, about the nature of the sign, about the identity of units of a language. We must begin by exploring Saussure's theory of language.

This is not an easy task. It requires detailed explication. That it is not an easy task is amply shown by the fact that Saussure himself did not feel in a position to write a course in general linguistics. If he had believed that he had solved the fundamental problems of linguistics in an unequivocal way, if he had not felt that he was still groping toward a satisfactory formulation of ideas which he but glimpsed, doubtless he would have written the book himself. Since he did not, we must make an effort to grasp a thought which is not yet fully born, but which, even in its nascent state, was able to exert a powerful influence on succeeding generations of linguists.

Our first task, therefore, after a brief look at Saussure's life and the circumstances that led to the publication of the *Course,* is to explore Saussure's theory of language: to begin with first principles and to reconstruct the foundations of modern linguistics. Thus equipped, we can undertake the second task which is essential if we are to understand Saussure and the significance of his work. The *Course* arose from Saussure's dissatisfaction with the theoretical foundations of linguistics as then practiced. What was the state of linguistics as Saussure saw it? How does his work fit in to the history of linguistics, the history of thought about language? Then, we can turn from the past to the present and future and outline the significance of Saussure's work for semiotics, the general science of signs which he envisaged but which did not really begin to take shape until many years after his death.

Following the fortunes of Saussure's ideas in linguistics and semiotics, tracing their actual influence, is doubtless our central task; but if we are to sum up his significance for twentieth-century thought, we must also attempt to bring into the open those aspects of his work which, inadequately formulated in the *Course,* have often been misconstrued or ignored. In this way we may try to insure that Saussure be considered not only an important figure of the recent past but also, and perhaps especially, a major intellectual presence today.

I

The Man and the *Course*

Saussure is a fascinating and enigmatic figure because he lived such an uneventful life. As far as we can tell, he had no great intellectual crises, decisive moments of insight or conversion, or momentous personal adventures. His own modesty about his thought, bold and uncompromising though that thought was, makes it very difficult to trace its genesis in his earlier intellectual life, and the fact that his major work should have remained unwritten seems the appropriate climax to this paradoxical career.

Born in Geneva in 1857, one year after Freud and one year before Durkheim, Saussure was the son of an eminent naturalist and member of a family with a strong tradition of accomplishment in the natural sciences. He was introduced to linguistic studies at an early age by Adolphe Pictet, a philologist and family friend. At the age of fifteen, after he had learned Greek to add to his French, German, English, and Latin, Saussure tried to work out a "general system of language," and wrote for Pictet an "Essay on Languages" in which he argued that all languages have their root in a system of two or three basic consonants. Pictet must have smiled at the extreme reductionism of this youthful attempt, but he did not discourage his protégé, who began to study Sanskrit while still at school.

Ferdinand de Saussure

In 1875 Saussure entered the University of Geneva but, following family tradition, enrolled as a student of physics and chemistry, though continuing to follow courses on Greek and Latin grammar. This experience convinced him that his career lay in the study of language, for not only did he join a professional linguistic association, the Linguistic Society of Paris, but, feeling that his first year at Geneva had been largely wasted, he persuaded his parents to send him to the University of Leipzig to study Indo-European languages.

Leipzig was a fortunate choice: it was the center for a school of young historical linguists, the *Junggrammatiker* ("Neogrammarians"), and for the first time Saussure was able to match wits with the most creative linguists of his day. His sense of his own powers was doubtless confirmed when one of his Leipzig teachers, Karl Brugmann, discovered what is called the law of *nasal sonans,* which Saussure had postulated several years earlier but rejected because it conflicted with the hypotheses of eminent linguists.

For four years Saussure remained in Leipzig, except for an interlude of eighteen months in Berlin, and in December 1878, when he was twenty-one, published his *Mémoire sur le système primitif des voyelles dans les langues indo-européennes* (Memoir on the Primitive System of Vowels in Indo-European Languages), which one linguist has called "the most splendid work of comparative philology ever written." The argument and conclusions of this work will be discussed later, but what is most striking about it is that the young linguist should have attacked a large and fundamental problem in historical linguistics and should have emphasized the importance of methodological problems. "I am not speculating," he wrote in his Preface, "on abstruse theoretical matters but inquiring into the very basis of the subject, without which everything is unanchored, arbitrary, and uncertain."

The *Mémoire* was well received in many quarters, and

when he returned to Leipzig from Berlin he was asked by one professor whether he was by any chance related to the great Swiss linguist, Saussure, the author of the *Mémoire*. However, Saussure seems to have found Germany uncongenial, and after defending his thesis on the use of the genitive case in Sanskrit (for which he was awarded his doctorate summa cum laude) he left for Paris.

In France, he was a considerable success. Soon after his arrival he began to teach Sanskrit, Gothic, and Old High German at the Ecole Pratique des Hautes Etudes and after 1887 expanded his teaching to cover Indo-European philology in general. He was active in the Linguistic Society of Paris and a major formative influence on the younger generation of French linguists. But in 1891, when offered a professorship at the University of Geneva, he decided to return to Switzerland, and even the honor which his older colleagues did him in having him named Chevalier de la Légion d'Honneur could not hold him in Paris.

In Geneva, his students were fewer and less advanced; he taught Sanskrit and historical linguistics generally. He married, fathered two sons, rarely traveled, and seemed to be settling into a decent provincial obscurity. He wrote less and less, and then painfully, reluctantly. In a letter of 1894, one of the few revealing personal documents we possess, he refers to an article which he has finally surrendered to an editor and continues:

> but I am fed up with all that, and with the general difficulty of writing even ten lines of good sense on linguistic matters. For a long time I have been above all preoccupied with the logical classification of linguistic facts and with the classification of the points of view from which we treat them; and I am more and more aware of the immense amount of work that would be required to show the linguist *what he is doing*. . . . The utter inadequacy of

current terminology, the need to reform it and, in order to do that, to demonstrate what sort of object language is, continually spoil my pleasure in philology, though I have no dearer wish than not to be made to think about the nature of language in general. This will lead, against my will, to a book in which I shall explain, without enthusiasm or passion, why there is not a single term used in linguistics which has any meaning for me. Only after this, I confess, will I be able to take up my work at the point I left off.[1]

He never wrote the book. He worked on Lithuanian, on medieval German legends, on a theory that Latin poets had concealed anagrams of proper names in their verses. But in 1906, on the retirement of another professor, the university assigned him responsibility for the teaching of general linguistics, and thenceforth, in alternate years (1907, 1908–9, 1910–11), he gave the lectures which were ultimately to become the *Course in General Linguistics*. In the summer of 1912 he fell ill and died in February 1913 at the age of fifty-six.

Saussure's career, though highly successful, was in no way extraordinary. His published writings would have assured him an honorable place in the history of philology, but a place roughly equivalent to that of other eminent Neogrammarians such as Brugmann and Verner, who are today known only to philologists. Fortunately, Saussure's students and colleagues thought that his work in general linguistics should be preserved, and they produced the volume which makes him a seminal thinker.

It was not an easy task. As Charles Bally and Albert Sechehaye recount in their preface to the *Course,* Saussure had

[1]Letter of 4 January 1894, in "Lettres de F. de Saussure à Antoine Meillet," *Cahiers Ferdinand de Saussure* 21 (1964), 95.

kept very few notes, so they had to work from notes taken by students who had attended the various series of lectures. But even when (from collation and comparison of notes) one gained a fair idea of what was said in each of the three lecture series, a major problem remained. To publish rough transcripts of all three series would involve enormous repetition (not to speak of inconsistencies), but to publish only one series would be to omit a good deal, since Saussure seemed to have composed each course afresh according to a different plan. Faced with this problem, Bally and Sechehaye, colleagues who had not themselves attended the lectures, made a bold decision that has been largely responsible for Saussure's influence. They decided to compose a unified work, to attempt a synthesis, granting precedence to the third series of lectures but drawing heavily on material from the other two and on Saussure's personal notes.

Most teachers would shudder at the thought of having their views handed on in this way, and it is indeed extraordinary that this unpromising procedure, fraught with possibilities of misunderstanding and compromise, should have produced a major work. But the fact is there: the *Course in General Linguistics,* as created by Bally and Sechehaye, is the source of Saussure's influence and reputation. Not until 1967, when Rudolf Engler began to publish the students' notes from which the *Course* was constructed, was it possible to go very far beyond the constructed text. It was the *Course* itself which influenced succeeding generations of linguists.

This fact poses something of a problem for our discussion. On the one hand, Saussure's importance in linguistics and in other fields rests less on what he "really" thought than on what is contained in the *Course.* On the other hand, the availability of the students' notes makes one wish to point out where the editors seem to have taken liberties, misunderstood, or falsified Saussure's thought. In general they did an admirable job, but there is a strong case for saying that in three respects they were less successful than one might have wished: their order of presentation is probably not that which Saussure would have chosen and thus does not reflect the potential logical sequence of his argument; the notion of the arbitrary nature of the sign receives much less discussion than it does in the notes; and in discussing the sound plane of language the editors are much less scrupulous and consistent in their terminology than Saussure seems to have been. These are important matters that one cannot wholly neglect, and thus in the discussion that follows, though I shall be primarily concerned with the *Course* itself, I shall occasionally attempt, especially through the order of presentation, to reconstruct more exactly what I take to be the logic of Saussure's thought. The major emphasis falls on the Saussurian teachings of the *Course* and their place in the history of linguistics, but in the exposition of Saussure's theory of language, to which we now turn, I shall not hesitate to rectify the original editors' occasional lapses.

2

Saussure's Theory of Language

Saussure was unhappy with linguistics as he knew it because he thought that his predecessors had failed to think se-
riously or perceptively about what they were doing. Linguistics, he wrote,[1] "never attempted to determine the nature of
the object it was studying, and without this elementary operation a science cannot develop an appropriate method"
(*Course*, 3; *Cours*, 16).

This operation is all the more necessary because human
language is an extremely complex and heterogeneous phenomenon. Even a single speech act involves an extraordinary
range of factors and could be considered from many different, even conflicting points of view. One could study the
way sounds are produced by the mouth, vocal chords, and
tongue; one could investigate the sound waves that are emit-
ted and the way they affect the hearing mechanism. One
could consider the signifying intention of the speaker, the aspects of the world to which his utterance refers, the immediate circumstances of the communicative context that might
have led him to produce a particular series of noises. One

[1] I use expressions such as "Saussure wrote" purely for convenience. As
was mentioned in Chapter 1, very few passages of the *Course* were actually
written by Saussure.

27

might try to analyze the conventions that enable speaker and listeners to understand one another, working out the grammatical and semantic rules that they must have assimilated if they are to communicate in this way. Or again, one could trace the history of the language that makes available these particular forms at this time.

Confronted with all these phenomena and these different perspectives from which one might approach them, the linguist must ask what one is trying to describe. What in particular is one looking at or looking for? What, in short, is language?

Saussure's answer to this question is unexceptionable but extremely important, since it serves to direct attention to essentials. Language is a system of signs. Noises count as language only when they serve to express or communicate ideas; otherwise they are just noise. And for noises to express or communicate ideas they must be part of a system of conventions that relate noises to ideas. They must, in other words, be part of a system of signs. The sign is the union of a form which signifies, which Saussure calls the *signifiant* (signifier), and an idea signified, the *signifié* (signified). Though we may speak of signifier and signified as if they were separate entities, they exist only as components of the sign. The sign is the central fact of language, and therefore in trying to separate what is essential from what is secondary or incidental we must start from the nature of the sign itself, its primary characteristics.

The Arbitrary Nature of the Sign

The first principle of Saussure's theory of language concerns the essential quality of the sign. The linguistic sign is arbitrary. A particular combination of signifier and signified is an arbitrary entity. This enigmatic principle, if properly understood, is central to one's conception of language and linguistic method.

> No one contests the principle of the arbitrary nature of the sign, but it is often easier to discover a truth than to assign it its rightful place. The above principle dominates the whole of linguistic analysis of a language. Its consequences are innumerable, though they are not all, it is true, equally evident right away. It is after many detours that one discovers them, and with them the fundamental importance of this principle. (*Course*, 68; *Cours*, 100)

What does Saussure mean by the arbitrary nature of the sign? In one sense the answer is quite simple. There is no natural or inevitable link between the signifier and the signified. Since I speak English I may use the signifier represented by *dog* to talk about an animal of a particular species, but this sequence of sounds is no better suited to that purpose than another sequence. *Lod, tet,* or *bloop* would serve equally well if it were accepted by members of my speech community. There is no intrinsic reason why one of these signifiers rather than another should be linked with the concept of a "dog." (Note that here, as throughout, I use italics to cite linguistic forms [e.g., *dog, lod*] and quotation marks to designate meanings [e.g., "dog"].)

Are there no exceptions to this basic principle? Certainly. There are two ways in which linguistic signs may be motivated, that is to say, made less arbitrary. First, there are cases of onomatopoeia, where the sound of the signifier seems in some way mimetic or imitative, as in the English *bow-wow* or *arf-arf* (cf. French *ouâ-ouâ*, German *wau-wau*, Italian *bau-bau*). But there are few such cases, and the fact that we identify them as a separate class and special case only emphasizes more strongly that ordinary signs are arbitrary.

However, within a particular language, signs may be partially motivated in a different way. The machine on which I am writing is called a *typewriter*. There is no intrinsic reason why it should not be called a *grue* or a *blimmel,* but, within English, *typewriter* is motivated because the meanings of the two sound sequences which compose its signifier, *type* and *writer,* are related to its signified, to the notion of a "typewriter." We might call this "secondary motivation." Notice, for example, that only in English is the relation between this sound sequence and the concept motivated. If the French were to use the same form to speak of this machine, that would be a wholly arbitrary sign, since the primary constituent, *writer* is not a sign in the French language. Moreover, for Saussure, as we shall see, the process of combining *type* and *writer* to create a new motivated sign is fundamentally similar to the way in which we combine words to form a phrase (whose meaning is related to the combined meanings of individual words). We can say, therefore, that languages have as their basic elements arbitrary signs. They then have various processes for combining these signs, but that does not alter the essential nature of language and its elementary constituents.

The sign is arbitrary in that there is no intrinsic link between signifier and signified. This is how Saussure's principle is usually interpreted, but in this form it is a wholly traditional notion, a rather obvious fact about language. Interpreted in this limited way, it does not have the momentous consequences which, according to the students' notes, Saussure repeatedly claimed for it: "the hierarchical place of this truth is at the very summit. It is only little by little that one recognizes how many different facts are but ramifications, hidden consequences of this truth" (Engler, 153). There is more to the arbitrary nature of the sign than the arbitrary relation between signifier and signified. We must push further.

From what I have said so far about signifier and signified,

one might be tempted to think of language as a nomenclature: a series of names arbitrarily selected and attached to a set of objects or concepts. It is, Saussure says, all too easy to think of language as a set of names and to make the biblical story of Adam naming the beasts an account of the very nature of language. If one says that the concept "dog" is rendered or expressed by *dog* in English, *chien* in French, and *Hund* in German, one implies that each language has an arbitrary name for a concept that exists prior to and independently of any language.

If language were simply a nomenclature for a set of universal concepts, it would be easy to translate from one language to another. One would simply replace the French name for a concept with the English name. If language were like this, the task of learning a new language would also be much easier than it is. But anyone who has attempted either of these tasks has acquired, alas, a vast amount of direct proof that languages are not nomenclatures, that the concepts or signifieds of one language may differ radically from those of another. The French "aimer" does not go directly into English; one must choose between "to like" and "to love." "Démarrer" includes in a single idea the English signifieds of "starting" and "accelerating." English "to know" covers the area of two French signifieds, "connaître" and "savoir." The English concepts of a "wicked" man and of a "pet" have no real counterparts in French. Or again, what English calls "light blue" and "dark blue" and treats as two shades of a single color are in Russian two distinct primary colors. Each language articulates or organizes the world differently. Languages do not simply name existing categories; they articulate their own.

Moreover, if language were a set of names applied to independently existing concepts, then in the historical evolution of a language the concepts should remain stable. Signifiers could evolve; the particular sequence of sounds associated with a given concept might be modified; and a given sequence of sounds could be attached to a different concept. Occasionally, of course, a new sign would have to be introduced for a new concept which had been produced by changes in the world. But the concepts themselves, as language-independent entities, would not be subject to linguistic evolution. In fact, though, the history of languages is full of examples of concepts shifting, changing their boundaries. The English word *cattle*, for example, at one point meant property in general, then gradually came to be restricted to four-footed property (a new category), and finally attained its modern sense of domesticated bovines. Or again, a "silly" person was once happy, blessed, and pious. Gradually this particular concept altered; the old concept of "silliness" transformed itself, and by the beginning of the sixteenth century a silly person was innocent, helpless, even deserving of pity. The alteration of the concept continued until, eventually, a silly person was simple, foolish, perhaps even stupid.

If language were a nomenclature we should be obliged to say that there exist a number of distinct concepts and that the signifier *silly* was attached first to one and then to another. But clearly this is not what happened: the concept attached to the signifier *silly* was continually shifting its boundaries, gradually changing its semantic shape, articulating the world in different ways from one period to the next. And, incidentally, the signifier also evolved, undergoing a modification of its central vowel.

What is the significance of this? What does it have to do with the arbitrary nature of the sign? Language is not a nomenclature and therefore its signifieds are not pre-existing concepts but changeable and contingent concepts which vary from one state of a language to another. And since the relation between signifier and signified is arbitrary, since there is no necessary reason for one concept rather than another to be attached to a given signifier, there is therefore no defining property which the concept must retain in order to count as the signified of that signifier. The signified associated with a signifier can take any form; there is no essential core of meaning that it must retain in order to count as the proper signified for that signifier. The fact that the relation between signifier and signified is arbitrary means, then, that since there are no fixed universal concepts or fixed universal signifiers, the signified itself is arbitrary, and so is the signifier. We then must ask, as Saussure does, what defines a signifier or a signified, and the answer leads us to a very important principle: both signifier and signified are purely relational or differential entities. Because they are arbitrary they are relational. This is a principle that requires explanation.

The Nature of Linguistic Units

Saussure attaches great importance—more so than it would appear from the published *Course*—to the fact that language is not a nomenclature, for unless we grasp this we cannot understand the full ramifications of the arbitrary nature of the sign. A language does not simply assign arbitrary names to a set of independently existing concepts. It sets up an arbitrary relation between signifiers of its own choosing on the one hand, and signifieds of its own choosing on the other. Not only does each language produce a different set of signifiers, articulating and dividing the continuum of sound in a distinctive way, but each language produces a different set of signifieds; it has a distinctive and thus "arbitrary" way of organizing the world into concepts or categories.

It is obvious that the sound sequences of *fleuve* and *rivière* are signifiers of French but not of English, whereas *river* and *stream* are English but not French. Less obviously, but more significantly, the organization of the conceptual plane is also different in English and French. The signified "river" is opposed to "stream" solely in terms of size, whereas a "fleuve" differs from a "rivière" not because it is necessarily larger but because it flows into the sea, while a "rivière" does not. In short, "fleuve" and "rivière" are not signifieds or concepts of English. They represent a different articulation of the conceptual plane.

The fact that these two languages operate perfectly well with different conceptual articulations or distinctions indicates that these divisions are not natural, inevitable, or necessary, but, in an important sense, arbitrary. Obviously it is important that a language have ways of talking about flowing bodies of water, but it can make its conceptual distinctions in this area in any of a wide variety of ways (size, swiftness of flow, straightness or sinuosity, direction of flow, depth, navigability, etc.). Not only can a language arbitrarily choose its signifiers; it can divide up a spectrum of conceptual possibilities in any way it likes.

Moreover, and here we come to an important point, the fact that these concepts, or signifieds, are arbitrary divisions of a continuum means that they are not autonomous entities, each of which is defined by some kind of essence. They are members of a system and are defined by their relations to the other members of that system. If I am to explain to someone the meaning of *stream* I must discuss the difference between a stream and a river, a stream and a rivulet, and so on. And, similarly, I cannot explain the French concept of a "rivière" without describing the distinction between "rivière" and "fleuve" on the one hand, and "rivière" and "ruisseau" on the other.

Color terms are a particularly good example of this characteristic of the sign. Suppose we wish to teach a foreigner about colors in English. Let us suppose also that this particular student is a rather slow learner and from a different culture, so that we must work out an efficient teaching strategy. It might occur to us that the best way to proceed would

34

be to take one color at a time: to begin, for example, with brown and not go on to another color until we were certain he had mastered brown. So we begin by showing him brown objects and telling him that they are brown. Since we want to be thorough, we have assembled a collection of a hundred brown objects of various kinds. Then, after having bored him and ourselves for several hours, we take him into another room and, to test his knowledge of "brown," ask him to pick out all the brown objects. He sets to work but seems to be having difficulty deciding what to select, so in despair we decide we haven't been thorough enough and propose to start again the next day with five hundred brown objects.

Fortunately, most of us would not adopt this desperate solution and would recognize what had gone wrong. However many brown objects we may show him, our pupil will not know the meaning of *brown,* and will not be able to pass our test, until we have taught him to distinguish between brown and red, brown and tan, brown and gray, brown and yellow, brown and black. It is only when he has grasped the relation between brown and other colors that he will begin to understand what brown is. And the reason for this is that "brown" is not an independent concept defined by some essential properties but one term in a system of color terms, defined by its relations with the other terms which delimit it.

Indeed, this painful teaching experience would bring us to understand that because the sign is arbitrary, because it is the result of dividing a continuum in ways peculiar to the language to which it belongs, we cannot treat the sign as an autonomous entity but must see it as part of a system. It is not just that in order to know the meaning of *brown* one must understand *red, tan, gray, black,* and so on. Rather, one could say that the signifieds of color terms are nothing but the product or result of a system of distinctions. Each language, in dividing the spectrum and distinguishing categories which it calls colors, produces a different system of signifieds:

units whose value depends on their relations with one another. As Saussure says, generalizing the point:

> in all cases, then, we discover not *ideas* given in advance but *values* emanating from the system. When we say that these values correspond to concepts, it is understood that these concepts are purely differential, not positively defined by their content but negatively defined by their relations with other terms of the system. Their most precise characteristic is that they are what the others are not. (*Course*, 117; *Cours*, 162)

Brown is what is not red, black, gray, yellow, etc., and the same holds for each of the other signifieds.

This is a major though paradoxical consequence of the arbitrary nature of the sign, and we shall return to it shortly. But perhaps the easiest way to grasp this notion of the purely relational nature of linguistic units is to approach it from another angle.

Consider the problem of identity in linguistics: the question of when two utterances or portions of an utterance count as examples of a single linguistic unit. Suppose someone tells me, "I bought a bed today," and I reply, "What sort of bed?" What do we mean when we say that the same sign has been employed twice in this brief conversation? What is the basis on which we can claim that two examples or instances of the same linguistic unit have appeared in our dialogue? Note that I have already begged the question in transcribing a portion of the noises that each of us made as *bed*. In fact, the actual noises which were produced will have been measurably different—different from a purely physical and acoustic point of view. Voices vary; after a very few words we can recognize a friend's voice on the telephone because the actual physical signals she emits are different from those of our other acquaintances.

My interlocutor and I produced different noises, yet we want to say that we have produced the same signifier, used the same sign. The signifier, then, is not the same thing as the noises that either he or I produced. It is an abstract unit of some kind, not to be confused with the actual sequence of sounds. But what sort of unit is it? Of what does the unit consist? We might approach this question by asking how far the actual noises produced could vary and still count as versions of the same signifier. This, of course, is similar to the question we implicitly asked about the signified: how far can a color vary and still count as brown? And the answer for the signifier is very similar to the answer for the signified. The noises made can vary considerably (there is no essential property which they must possess), so long as they do not become confused with those of contrasting signifiers. We have considerable latitude in the way we utter *bed*, so long as what we say is not confused with *bad, bud, bid, bode; bread, bled, dead, fed, head, led, red, said, wed; beck, bell, bet.*

In other words, it is the distinctions which are important, and it is for this reason that linguistic units have a purely relational identity. The principle is not easy to grasp, but Saussure offers a concrete analogy. We are willing to grant that in an important sense the 8:25 Geneva-to-Paris Express is the same train each day, even though the coaches, locomotive, and personnel change from one day to the next. What gives the train its identity is its place in the system of trains, as indicated by the timetable. And note that this relational identity is indeed the determining factor: the train remains the same train even if it leaves a half-hour late. In fact, it might always leave late without ceasing to be the 8:25 Geneva-to-Paris Express. What is important is that it be distinguished from, say, the 10:25 Geneva-to-Paris Express, the 8:40 Geneva-to-Dijon Local, and so on.

Another analogy Saussure uses to illustrate the notion of relational identity is the comparison between language and chess. The basic units of chess are obviously king, queen, rook, knight, bishop, and pawn. The actual physical shape of the pieces and the material from which they are made is of no importance. The king may be of any size and shape, as long as there are ways of distinguishing it from other pieces. The two rooks need not be of identical size and shape, so long as they can be distinguished from other pieces. Thus, as Saussure points out, if a piece is lost from a chess set we can replace it with any other sort of object, provided always that this object will not be confused with the objects representing pieces of a different value (*Course,* 110; *Cours,* 153–54). The actual physical properties of pieces are of no importance, so long as there are differences of some kind—any kind will do—between pieces which have a different value.

Thus one can say that the units of the game of chess have no material identity: there are no physical properties necessary to a king or pawn. Identity is wholly a function of differences within a system. If we now apply the analogy to language we shall be in a position to understand Saussure's paradoxical claim that in the system of a language "there are only differences, with no positive terms" (*Course,* 120; *Cours,* 166). Normally, when we think of differences we presuppose two things that differ, but Saussure's point is that signifier and signified are not things in this sense. Just as we cannot say anything about what a pawn must look like, except that it will be different from knight, rook, and so on, so the signifier which we represent as *bed* is not defined by any particular noises used in uttering it. Not only do the actual noises differ from one case to another, but English could be arranged so that noises now used to express the signifier *pet* were used for the signifier *bed,* and vice versa. If these changes were made, the units of the language would be expressed differently; but they would still be fundamentally the same units (the same differences remain, both on the level of the signifier and on the level of the signified), and the language would still be English. Indeed, English would remain, in an important sense, the same language if the units of the signifier were never expressed in sound but only in visual symbols of some kind.

In saying this I am obviously making a distinction between units of the linguistic system and their actual physical manifestations or realizations. Before discussing this very important distinction in greater detail, it may be useful to recapitulate the line of reasoning that led to it. We began by noting that there was no natural link between signifier and signified, and then, trying to explain the arbitrary nature of the linguistic sign, we saw that both signifier and signified were arbitrary divisions or delimitations of a continuum (a sound spectrum on the one hand and a conceptual field on the other). This led us to infer that both signifier and signified must be defined in terms of their relations with other signifiers and signifieds, and thus we reached the conclusion that if we are to define the units of a language, we must distinguish between these purely relational and abstract units and their physical realizations. The actual sounds we produce in speaking are not in themselves units of the linguistic system, nor is the physical color which we designate in calling a book "brown" the same thing as the linguistic unit (the signified, or concept) "brown." In both cases, and this is a point on which Saussure rightly insists, the linguistic unit is form rather than substance, defined by the relations that set it off from other units.

Langue and *Parole*

Here, in the distinction between the linguistic system and its actual manifestations, we have reached the crucial opposition between *langue* and *parole*. *La langue* is the system of a language, the language as a system of forms, whereas *parole* is actual speech, the speech acts that are made possible by the language. *La langue* is what individuals assimilate when they learn a language, a set of forms or "hoard deposited by the practice of speech in speakers who belong to the same community, a grammatical system which, to all intents and purposes, exists in the mind of each speaker" (*Course*, 13–14; *Cours*, 30). "It is the social product whose existence permits the individual to exercise his linguistic faculty" (Engler, 31). *Parole,* on the other hand, is the "executive side of language," and for Saussure involves both "the combinations by which the speaker uses the code of the linguistic system in order to express his own thoughts" and "the psychophysical mechanisms which permit him to externalize these combinations" (*Course*, 14; *Cours*, 31). In the act of *parole* the speaker selects and combines elements of the linguistic system and gives these forms a concrete phonic and psychological manifestion, as sounds and meanings.

If these remarks on *parole* seem somewhat confusing it is because they contain a problem, to which we shall return. If the combination of linguistic elements belongs to *parole,* then syntactic rules have an ambiguous status. To make *la langue* a system of forms and *parole* the combination and externalization of these forms is not quite the same as making *langue* the linguistic faculty and *parole* the exercise of that faculty, for the linguistic faculty includes knowledge of how to combine elements, rules of combination. This latter distinction, between *langue* as system and *parole* as realization, is the more fundamental, both in Saussure and in the Saussurian tradition. However, it is not essential to define here the specific characteristics of *parole,* since, as Saussure makes clear, the principal and strategic function of the distinction between *langue* and *parole* is to isolate the object of linguistic investigation. *La langue,* Saussure argued, must be the linguist's primary concern. What one is trying to do in analyzing a language is not to describe speech acts but to determine the units and rules of combination which make up the linguistic system. *La langue,* or the linguistic system, is a coherent, analyzable object; "it is a system of signs in which the only essential thing is the union of meanings and acoustic images" (*Course,* 15; *Cours,* 32). In studying language as a system of signs, one is trying to identify its essential features: those elements which are crucial to the signifying function of language or, in other words, the elements which are functional within the system in that they create signs by distinguishing them one from another.

The distinction between *langue* and *parole* thus provides a principle of relevance for linguistics. "In separating *langue* from *parole,*" Saussure writes, "we are separating what is social from what is individual and what is essential from what is ancillary or accidental" (*Course,* 14; *Cours,* 30). If we tried to study everything related to the phenomenon of speech we would enter a realm of confusion where relevance and irrelevance were extremely difficult to determine; but if we concentrate on *la langue,* then various aspects of language and speech fall into place within or around it. Once we put forward this notion of the linguistic system, then we can ask of every phenomenon whether it belongs to the system itself or is simply a feature of the performance or realization of linguistic units, and we thus succeed in classifying speech facts into groups in which they can profitably be studied.

For example, the distinction between *langue* and *parole* leads to the creation of two distinct disciplines that study sound and its linguistic functions: phonetics, which studies sound in speech acts from a physical point of view, and phonology, which is not interested in physical events themselves but in the distinctions between the abstract units of the signifier which are functional within the linguistic system. (It is important to note here that although Saussure states unequivocally that physical sounds themselves are not part of *la langue* and thus paves the way for the distinction between phonetics and phonology as defined above, he himself uses the terms *phonetics* and *phonology* in a very different sense. I shall continue to use them in the modern sense defined here.)

The distinction between phonetics and phonology takes us back to points made earlier about the linguistic identity of the form *bed*. Phonetics would describe the actual sounds produced when one utters the form, but, as we argued above, the identity of *bed* as a unit of English does not depend on the nature of these actual sounds but on the distinctions which separate *bed* from *bet, bad, head,* etc. Phonology is the study of these functional distinctions, and "functional" is what should be stressed here. For example, in English utterances there is a perceptible and measurable difference between the "l-sound" that occurs before vowels (as in *lend* or *alive*) and that which occurs before consonants or at the end of words (as in *melt or peel*). This is a real phonetic difference, but it is not a difference ever used to distinguish between two signs. It is not a functional difference and therefore is not a part of the phonological system of English. On the other hand, the difference between the vowels of *feel* and *fill* is used in English to distinguish signs (compare *keel* and *kill, keen* and *kin, seat* and *sit, heat* and *hit,* and the like). This opposition plays a very important role in the phonological system of English in that it creates a large number of distinct signs.

The same distinction between what belongs to particular linguistic acts and what belongs to the linguistic system itself is important at other levels too, not just that of sound. We can distinguish, for example, between utterance, as a unit of *parole,* and sentence, a unit of *la langue.* Two different utterances may be manifestations of the same sentence; so once again we encounter this central notion of identity in linguistics. The actual sounds and the contextual meanings of the two utterances will be different; what makes the two utterances instances of a single linguistic unit will be the distinctions which give that unit a relational identity.

For example, if at some time Cuthbert says "I am tired," *I* refers to Cuthbert, and understanding this reference is an important part of understanding the utterance. However, that reference is not part of the meaning of the sentence, for George also may utter the same sentence, and in his utterance *I* will refer to George. Within the linguistic system, *I* does not refer to anyone. Its meaning in the system is the result of the distinctions between *I* and *you, he, she, it, we,* and *they:* a meaning which we can sum up by saying that *I* means "the speaker" as opposed to anyone else.

Pronouns are obvious illustrations of the difference between meanings which pertain to utterances only, and meanings which pertain to elements of the linguistic system. To characterize this distinction Saussure uses the terms *signification* and *valeur* ("value"). Linguistic units have a value within the system, a meaning which is the result of the oppositions that define them; but when these units are used in an utterance, they have a signification, a contextual realization or manifestation of meaning. For example, if a French speaker says "J'ai vu un mouton" and an English speaker says "I saw a sheep" their utterances are likely to have the same signification; they are making the same claim about a state of affairs (namely, that at a time in the past the speaker saw a sheep). However, as units of their respective linguistic systems, *mouton* and *sheep* do not have the same meaning or value, for "sheep" is defined by an opposition with "mutton," whereas *"mouton"* is bounded by no such distinction but is used both for the animal and for the meat. There are certain philosophical problems here that Saussure did not tackle; in particular, philosophers would want to say that what Saussure calls the signification of an utterance involves both meaning and reference. But Saussure's point is that there is one kind of meaning, a relational meaning or value, which is based on the linguistic system, and another kind of meaning or signification which involves the use of linguistic elements in actual situations of utterance.

The distinction between *langue* and *parole* has important

consequences for other disciplines besides linguistics, for it is essentially a distinction between institution and event, between the underlying system that makes possible various types of behavior and actual instances of such behavior. Study of the system leads to the construction of models that represent forms, their relations to one another, and their possibilities of combination, whereas study of actual behavior or events would lead to the construction of statistical models that represent the probabilities of particular combinations under various circumstances.

In our discussion of semiotics in chapter 4 we shall see how the notion of *langue* has been extended to other fields. Within linguistics itself, though, study of *la langue* involves an inventory of the distinctions that create signs and of rules of combination, whereas study of *parole* would lead to an account of language use, including the relative frequencies with which particular forms or combinations of forms were used in actual speech. By separating *langue* from *parole* Saussure gave linguistics a suitable object of study and thus a much clearer sense of what it was doing: if one focused on language as a system, then one knew what one was trying to reconstruct and could, within this perspective, determine what evidence was relevant and how it should be organized.

We shall consider in more detail the structure of the linguistic system, but there is one point about the concept of *la langue* which should be stressed here. Saussure's editors organized the *Course* so that it began with the distinction between *langue* and *parole*. Saussure was thus portrayed as saying that language is a confused mass of heterogeneous facts, and the only way to make sense of it is to postulate the existence of something called the linguistic system and to set aside everything else. The distinction has thus seemed extremely questionable to many people: a postulate that had to be accepted on faith if one were to proceed. But in fact, as Saussure's notes suggest and as the sequence of argument which we have adopted here should have demonstrated, the distinction between *langue* and *parole* is a logical and necessary consequence of the arbitrary nature of the sign and the problem of identity in linguistics. In brief: if the sign is arbitrary then, as we have seen, it is a purely relational entity, and if we wish to define and identify signs we must look to the system of relations and distinctions which create them. We must therefore distinguish between the various substances in which signs are manifested and the actual forms which constitute signs; and when we do this what we have isolated is a system of forms which underlies actual linguistic behavior or manifestation. This system of forms is *la langue;* the attempt to study signs leads us, inexorably, to take this as the proper object of linguistic investigation. The isolation of *la langue* is not, as the published *Course* may suggest, an arbitrary point of departure but a consequence of the nature of signs themselves.

Synchronic and Diachronic Perspectives

There is another important consequence of the arbitrary nature of the sign which has also been treated by Saussure's critics as a questionable and unnecessary imposition. This is the distinction between the *synchronic* study of language (study of the linguistic system in a particular state, without reference to time) and the *diachronic* study of language (study of its evolution in time). It has been suggested that in distinguishing rigorously between these two perspectives and in granting priority to the synchronic study of language, Saussure was ignoring, or at least setting aside, the fact that a language is fundamentally historical and contingent, an entity in constant evolution. But, on the contrary, it was precisely because he recognized, more profoundly than his critics, the radical historicity of language that he asserted the importance of dis-

45

tinguishing between facts about the linguistic system and facts about linguistic evolution, even in cases where the two kinds of facts seem extraordinarily intertwined. There is an apparent paradox here and it requires elucidation.

What is the connection between the arbitrary nature of the sign and the profoundly historical nature of language? We can put it in this way: if there were some essential or natural connection between signifier and signified, then the sign would have an essential core which would be unaffected by time or which at least would resist change. This unchanging essence could be opposed to those "accidental" features which did alter from one period to another. But, in fact, as we have seen, there is no aspect of the sign which is a necessary property and which therefore lies outside time. Any aspect of sound or meaning can alter; the history of languages is full of radical evolutionary alterations of both sound and meaning. The Old English *þing,* meaning "discussion," has gradually become the modern English *thing* with a totally different meaning. The Greek *Θηριαχός* (theriakos), meaning "pertaining to a wild animal," became the modern English *treacle.* The Latin *calidum* ("hot") became the modern French *chaud* (pronounced ʃo, as in English *show*), in which meaning persists but none of the original phonological elements are preserved. In short, neither signifier nor signified contains any essential core that time cannot touch. Because it is arbitrary, the sign is totally subject to history, and the combination at a particular moment of a given signifier and signified is a contingent result of the historical process.

The fact that the sign is arbitrary or wholly contingent makes it subject to history but also means that signs require an ahistorical analysis. This is not as paradoxical as it might seem. Since the sign has no necessary core that must persist, it must be defined as a relational entity, in its relations to other signs. And the relevant relations are those which obtain at a particular time. A language, Saussure says, "is a system of pure values which are determined by nothing except the momentary arrangement of its terms" (*Course,* 80; *Cours,* 116). Because the language is a wholly historical entity, always open to change, one must focus on the relations that exist in a particular synchronic state if one is to define its elements.

In asserting the priority of synchronic description, Saussure is pointing out the irrelevance of historical or diachronic facts to the analysis of *la langue.* Some examples will show why diachronic information is irrelevant. In modern English the second-person pronoun *you* is used to refer both to one person and to many and can be either the subject or object in a sentence. In an earlier state of the language, however, *you* was defined by its opposition to *ye* on the one hand (*ye* a subject pronoun and *you* an object pronoun) and to *thee* and *thou* on the other (*thee* and *thou* singular forms and *you* a plural form). At a later stage *you* came to serve also as a respectful way of addressing one person, like the modern French *vous.* Now in modern English *you* is no longer defined by its opposition to *ye, thee,* and *thou.* One can know and speak modern English perfectly without knowing that *you* was once a plural and objective form, and indeed, if one knows this, there is no way in which this knowledge can serve as part of one's knowledge of modern English. The description of modern English *you* would remain exactly the same if its historical evolution had been wholly different, for *you* in modern English is defined by its role in the synchronic state of the language.

Similarly, the French noun *pas* ("step") and the negative adverb *pas* ("not") derive historically from a single sign, but this is irrelevant to a description of modern French, where the two words function in totally different ways and must be treated as distinct signs. It makes no difference in modern French whether these two signs were once, as is in fact the case, a single sign, or whether they were once totally distinct signs whose different signifiers have become similar through sound changes (this has happened, for example, with the English *skate,* where sound changes have brought together the fish *skate,* from Old Norse *skata,* and ice *skate,* from Dutch *schaats*). To try to incorporate these historical facts into an account of the contemporary linguistic system would be a distortion and falsification.

Saussure's insistence on the difference between synchronic and diachronic perspectives and on the priority of synchronic description does not mean, however, that he had deceived himself into thinking that language exists as a series of totally homogeneous synchronic states: English of 1920, English of 1940, English of 1960. In a sense, the notion of a synchronic state is a methodological fiction. When we talk about the linguistic system of French at a given time we are abstracting from a reality which consists of a very large number of native speakers, whose linguistic systems may differ in various ways. Nevertheless, the linguistic system of French is a definite reality, in that all these speakers understand one another, whereas someone who speaks only English cannot understand them. Since we want to represent this fact and speak of the system which these native speakers have in common, we produce statements about the linguistic system in a particular synchronic state.

Moreover, even if the notion of a synchronic state is a methodological fiction, it is important to remember that statements about the historical evolution of language are equally fictitious. Suppose I wished to make the diachronic claim that in twentieth-century French the sound /ɑ/ has become /a/ (I follow here the convention of placing phonological forms between oblique lines). What does this mean? To say that /ɑ/ became /a/ suggests the transformation of an object in time, but in fact this is a historical fiction which summarizes a lot of synchronic facts: that at an earlier point in the century there were many speakers who distinguished between two *a*'s, as in *pâte* and *patte* or *tâche* and *tache,* whereas now there are few speakers who make the distinction, so that there is coming to be only one *a* in the language. Even this, of course, may be an oversimplification in that some speakers will hear the distinction but not use it themselves, whereas others will use it only in relatively formal circumstances.

As this example shows, a diachronic statement relates a single element from one state of a linguistic system to an element from a later state of the system. Given the relational nature of linguistic units, the fact that they are wholly defined by relations within their own state of the system, this is a questionable thing to do, foreign to the principle of synchronic linguistics. How can it be justified? How can one postulate a diachronic identity?

Saussure argues that despite their different status, diachronic statements are derived from synchronic statements. What allows us, he asks, to state the fact that Latin *mare* became French *mer* ("sea")? The historical linguist might argue that we know *mare* became *mer* because here, as elsewhere, the final *e* was dropped and *a* became *e*. But, Saussure argues, to suggest that these regular sound changes are what create the link between the two forms is to get things backward, because what enables us to identify this sound change is our initial notion that one form became the other. "We are using the correspondence between *mare* and *mer* to decide that *a* became *e* and that final *e* fell" (*Course*, 182; *Cours*, 249).

In fact, what we are supposing in connecting *mare* and *mer* is this: that *mare, mer,* and the intermediate forms constitute an unbroken chain of synchronic identities. At each period where, retrospectively, we can say that a change occurred, there was an old form and a new form which were phonetically different but phonologically or functionally identical. They may of course have had different associations (e.g., one form might have seemed a bit old-fashioned) but they could be used interchangeably by speakers. No doubt some would

49

stick to the old form and others prefer the new, but since the move from one to the other would not produce a difference in actual meaning, from the point of view of the linguistic system there would be a synchronic identity between the two forms. It is in this sense that diachronic identity depends on a series of synchronic identities.

As Saussure says with respect to another example, "the diachronic identity of two words as different as *calidum* and *chaud* ("hot") means simply that one passed from the former to the latter through a series of synchronic identities" (*Course*, 182; *Cours*, 250). At one point *calidum* and *calidu* were interchangeable and synchronically identical, then later *calidu* and *caldu*, then *caldu* and *cald*, then *cald* and *tʃalt*, then *tʃalt* and *tʃaut*, then *tʃaut* and *ʃaut*, then *ʃaut* and *ʃot*, and finally *ʃot* and *ʃo* (the pronunciation of *chaud*). When we speak of the transformation of a word and postulate a diachronic identity, we are in fact summarizing a parleyed series of synchronic identities. "This is why I said," Saussure continues, "that knowing why 'Gentlemen!' retains its identity when repeated several times during a lecture is just as interesting as knowing . . . why *chaud* is identical to *calidum*. The second problem is in fact only an extension and complication of the first" (*Course*, 182; *Cours*, 250).

Thus, one cannot argue that diachronic linguistics is in some way closer to the reality of language, while synchronic analysis is a fiction. Historical filiations are derived from synchronic identities. Not only that: they are facts of a different order. Synchronically speaking, diachronic identities are a distortion, for the earlier and later signs which they relate have no common properties. Each sign has no properties other than the specific relational properties which define it within its own synchronic system. From the point of view of systems of signs, which after all is the point of view that matters when dealing with signs, the earlier and later signs are wholly disparate.

Whence the importance of separating the synchronic and diachronic perspectives, even when the facts they are treating seem inextricably intertwined. This is a point one must stress, because linguists who oppose Saussure's radical distinction between synchronic and diachronic approaches and wish to envisage a synthetic, panchronic perspective, often point to the entanglement of synchronic and diachronic facts as if it supported their case. Saussure is all too aware of the intertwining of synchronic and diachronic facts; indeed, for him the whole difficulty is one of separating these elements when they are mixed, because only in this way can linguistic analysis attain coherence. Linguistic forms have synchronic and diachronic aspects which must be separated because they are facts of a different order, with different conditions of existence.

A panchronic synthesis is impossible, Saussure argues, because of the arbitrary nature of linguistic signs. In other sorts of systems, one might hold together the synchronic and diachronic perspectives: "insofar as a value is rooted in things themselves and in their natural relations, one can, to a certain extent, follow this value through time, bearing in mind that it depends at each moment on a system of values that coexist with it" (*Course,* 80; *Cours,* 116). Thus, the value of a piece of land at a given moment will depend on a great many other factors in the economic system, but the value is somewhat rooted in the nature of the land itself and variations will not involve simply the replacement of one arbitrary value by another. But in the case of language, where the value of a sign has no natural basis or inherent limits, historical change has a different character. Elements of a language, Saussure says, "are abandoned to their own historical evolution in a way that is wholly unknown in areas where forms have the smallest degree of natural connection with meaning" (Engler, 169). Since no signifier is naturally more suited to a signified than any other, sound change takes place independently of the system of values: "a diachronic fact is an event with its own rationale; the particular synchronic consequences which may follow from it are completely foreign to it" (*Course*, 84; *Cours*, 121).

Saussure's argument here is a complicated one. The claim is that diachronic facts are of a different order from synchronic facts in that historical change originates outside the linguistic system. Change originates in linguistic performance, in *parole*, not in *la langue*, and what is modified are individual elements of the system of realization. Historical changes affect the system in the end, in that the system will adjust to them, make use of the results of historical change, but it is not the linguistic system which produces them.

One thing Saussure is opposing here is the notion of teleology in linguistics: the idea that there is some end toward which linguistic changes are working and that they take place in order to achieve that end. Changes do not occur *in order to* produce a new state of the system. What happens is that "certain elements are altered without regard to their solidarity within the system as a whole."[2] These isolated changes have general consequences for the system, in that its network of relations will be altered. However, "it is not that one system has produced another but that an element of the first has been changed, and that has sufficed to bring into existence another system" (*Course*, 85; *Cours*, 121). Changes are part of an independent evolutionary process to which the system adjusts.

A diachronic fact involves the displacement of one form by another. This displacement does not in itself have any signifi-

[2]An important exception, which Saussure discusses at length but which I here leave aside, is the phenomenon known as "analogy," in which new forms are created on the analogy of existing forms. This is an important factor in linguistic change, but Saussure argues that it is fundamentally a synchronic phenomenon. For discussion see Chapter 3, pp. 80–81.

cance; from the point of view of the linguistic system, it is nonfunctional. A synchronic fact is a relationship or opposition between two forms existing simultaneously: a relationship which is significant in that it carries meaning within the language. Whenever linguistic change has repercussions for the system, one will have a situation where both sorts of facts are mixed together and are easy to confuse. But they are very different and must be separated. In order to grasp the difference and its importance, let us consider some English nouns with unusual plural forms: *feet, geese, teeth*. What are the synchronic and diachronic aspects of the development of these forms?

In early Anglo-Saxon, the singular and plural forms of these nouns seem to have been as follows:

Stage One

	singular	*plural*	
foot:	fōt	fōti	(pronounced roughly *foat, foati*)
goose:	gōs	gōsi	
tooth:	tōþ	tōþi	(where þ = th)

Then, plural forms were affected by a phonetic change known as "*i* mutation": when *i* followed a stressed syllable, the vowel of the stressed syllable was affected, and back vowels were fronted, so that ō became ē. This gave:

Stage Two

	singular	*plural*
foot:	fōt	fēti
goose:	gōs	gēsi
tooth:	tōþ	tēþi

Then, in a second phonetic change, the final *i* was dropped, and gave:

53

Stage Three

	singular	*plural*
foot:	fōt	fēt
goose:	gōs	gēs
tooth:	tōþ	tēþ

These forms, by the Great English Vowel Shift in which ō became ū and ē became ī, then became the modern forms (*Course*, 83–84; *Cours*, 120).

At stage one, the plural was marked by the presence of a final *i*. This is a synchronic fact: that the opposition between presence and absence of *i* marked the opposition between singular and plural. Then, a phonetic change, which had nothing to do with plurals or indeed with the grammar of the language at all, brought about a change in those forms containing a final *i*. This change had nothing to do with plurals (nothing to do with the synchronic opposition between singular and plural) in that it occurred wherever *i* followed a stressed syllable—even in verbs, for example. But, as it happened, a certain number of plural forms were affected, producing a new synchronic fact in stage two. Some plural forms, as a result of an event which had nothing to do with plurals as such, had come to be marked by a double opposition: between the presence and absence of a final *i*, as before, and between the *e* of the plural and the *o* of the singular. Then, with the fall of final *i*, which again did not concern plurals as such, there came to be a new synchronic situation. The shape of the plural forms had changed through a historical event, but since there was still a difference between the singular and plural forms (*o* as opposed to *e*) the linguistic system was able to use this difference as a meaning-bearing opposition.

"This observation" Saussure writes, "helps us to understand more fully the fortuitous nature of a linguistic state. . . . The state which resulted from the change was not designed to

54

signal the meanings with which it has been endowed. A fortuitous state was given (*fōt : fēt*); and speakers took it over to make it carry the distinction between singular and plural. *Fōt : fēt* is no better suited to this purpose than *fōt : fōti*. In each state mind breathes life into a substance which is given" (*Course*, 85; *Cours*, 121–22). From the point of view of the linguistic system, the significant facts are the synchronic ones. Diachronic events throw up new forms which then become part of a new system, but, as Saussure says, "in the diachronic perspective one is dealing with phenomena which are unrelated to the systems, though they condition them" (*Course*, 85; *Cours*, 122).

Saussure urges the necessity of distinguishing the synchronic and diachronic perspectives in all cases, but his discussion treats only sound changes. Of course, the examples he discusses do have morphological and grammatical consequences within the system, and such readjustments may eventually have semantic consequences, but he never deals with the problem of semantic change itself, the diachronic alterations of signifieds. He admits, in passing, that once one leaves the plane of sound it becomes more difficult to maintain the absolute distinction between the synchronic and the diachronic (*Course*, 141; *Cours*, 194); but the theory certainly enjoins one to do so, and one can make out a plausible though unfashionable case for the extension of the distinction to semantics.

The argument is formally very similar to that involving sound changes. Suppose one were studying the change in meaning of *Kunst* in Middle High German between roughly 1200 and 1300. What would be synchronic and what diachronic here? To define change of meaning one needs two meanings and these can be determined only by considering synchronic facts: the relations between signifieds in a given state of the language which define the semantic area of "kunst." At an early stage it was a higher, courtly knowledge or competence, as opposed to lower, more technical skills ("list"), and a partial accomplishment as opposed to the synoptic wisdom of "wîsheit." In a later stage the two major oppositions which defined it were different: mundane versus spiritual ("wîsheit") and technical ("wizzen") versus nontechnical. What we have are two different organizations of a semantic field. A diachronic statement would be based on this synchronic information, but if it were to explain what happened to "kunst" it would have to refer to nonlinguistic factors or causes (social changes, psychological processes, etc.) whose effects happened to have repercussions for the semantic system. For analysis of the language the relevant facts are the synchronic oppositions. The diachronic perspective treats individual filiations, which are identifiable only from the results of synchronic analysis, and draws upon what Stephen Ullmann calls "the infinite variety and complexity of causes which govern semantic change" in order to account for the move from one state to another. But a knowledge of previous meanings and of the particular causes of change would not be relevant to an account of the semantic relations of a synchronic state (except insofar as previous meanings were still present in the system, in which case they would be considered synchronically, not diachronically).

Here, as in the cases which Saussure considers, diachronic facts are of a different order from the synchronic, bearing on individual elements rather than on the system, which alone can define those elements as linguistic units. History, the historical evolution of individual elements, throws up forms that the system uses, and the study of those systematic uses is the central task. Historical or causal explanation is not what is required; it bears on the elements of a language, not the language, and bears on them only as elements. Explanation in linguistics is structural: one explains forms and rules of combination by setting out the underlying system of relations, in a particular synchronic state, which create and define the elements of that synchronic system.

Analysis of *La Langue*

The two major consequences of the arbitrary nature of the sign, which we have now explored, both point to a single fact, which may be considered the center of Saussure's theory of language: language is form, not substance. A language is a system of mutually related values, and to analyze the language is to set out the system of values which constitute a state of the language. As opposed to the positive phonic and signifying elements of speech acts, or *parole, la langue* is a system of oppositions or differences, and the task of the analyst is to discover what are these functional differences.

The basic problem, as we have followed Saussure in insisting, is that of linguistic identity. Nothing is given in linguistics. There are no positive, self-defined elements with which to start. In order to identify two instances of the same unit, we must construct a formal and relational entity by distinguishing between differences which are nonfunctional (and hence, for Saussure, nonlinguistic) and differences which are functional. Once we have identified the relations and oppositions which delimit signifiers on the one hand, and signifieds on the other, we have things we may speak of as positive entities, linguistic signs, though we must remember that they are entities which emerge from and depend on the network of differences that constitutes the linguistic system at a given time.

But, so far, in speaking of signs or linguistic units, it may sound as though we were speaking of words only, as if language consisted of nothing more than a vocabulary, organized according to phonological and semantic oppositions.

Naturally language consists also of many grammatical relations and distinctions, but Saussure insists, in a passage that is worth quoting at length, that there is no fundamental difference between a linguistic unit and a grammatical fact. Their common nature is a result of the fact that signs are entirely differential objects and that what constitutes a linguistic sign (of whatever kind) is nothing but differences between signs.

"A rather paradoxical consequence of this principle is that, in the final analysis, what is commonly referred to as a 'grammatical fact' fits our definition of a linguistic unit." It is always expressed by an opposition between terms. Thus, in the case of the German opposition between *Nacht* ("night") and *Nächte* ("nights") it is the difference which carries grammatical meaning.

> Each of the terms present in the grammatical fact (the singular without umlaut and final *e*, as opposed to the plural with umlaut and final *e*) is itself the result of the interplay of oppositions within the system. Taken by itself, neither *Nacht* nor *Nächte* is anything; thus everything lies in the opposition. In other words, one could express the relationship between *Nacht* and *Nächte* by an algebraic formula *a/b*, where *a* and *b* are not simple terms but are themselves each the result of a set of oppositions. The linguistic system is, as it were, an algebra which contains only complex terms. Among its oppositions some are more significant than others, but "linguistic unit" and "grammatical fact" are only different names for designating aspects of the same general phenomenon: the play of linguistic oppositions. So true is this that we could approach the problem of linguistic units by starting with grammatical facts. Taking an opposition like *Nacht : Nächte,* we could ask what are the units involved in this opposition? Are they these two

words only, or the whole series of similar words? or *a* and *ä*, or all singulars and plurals, and so forth?

Linguistic unit and grammatical fact would not be similar to one another if linguistic signs were made up of something besides differences. But the linguistic system being what it is, wherever one begins one will find nothing simple, but always and everywhere this same complex equilibrium of reciprocally defined or conditioned terms. In other words, language is a form and not a substance. One cannot steep oneself too deeply in this truth, for all the mistakes in our terminology, all our incorrect ways of designating aspects of language, come from this involuntary assumption that linguistic phenomena must have substance. (*Course,* 121–22; *Cours,* 168–69)

Consider, for example, the case of the English word *took.* What is the sign of the past tense here? It is obviously nothing positive in the word itself but a relational element. The opposition between *take* and *took* carries the distinction between present and past, just as the opposition between *foot* and *feet* carries the distinction of number. Without *feet, foot* would presumably be indeterminate, just as *sheep* is (cf. "I saw the sheep in the field"). Grammatical facts illustrate the purely relational nature of the sign and confirm Saussure's radical conception of the "fundamentally identical nature of all synchronic facts" (*Course,* 134; *Cours,* 187).

In studying a language, then, the linguist is concerned with relationships: identities and differences. One discovers, Saussure argues, two major types of relationship. On the one hand, there are those which we have so far been discussing: oppositions which produce distinct and alternative terms (*b* as opposed to *p; foot* as opposed to *feet*). On the other hand, there are the relations between units which combine to form sequences. In a linguistic sequence, a term's value depends not only on the contrast between it and the others that might have been chosen in its stead but also on its relations with the terms that precede and follow it in sequence. The former, which Saussure calls *associative* relations, are now generally called *paradigmatic* relations. The latter are called *syntagmatic* relations. Syntagmatic relations define combinatory possibilities: the relations between elements that might combine in a sequence. Paradigmatic relations are the oppositions between elements that can replace one another.

These relations hold at various levels of linguistic analysis. Thus, the phoneme /p/ in English is defined both by its opposition to other phonemes that could replace it in contexts such as /_et/ (cf. *bet, let, met, net, set*), and by its combinatory relations with other phonemes (it can precede or follow any vowel; within a syllable the liquids /l/ and /r/ are the only consonants that can follow it and /s/ the only one that can precede it).

At the level of morphology or word structure we also find both syntagmatic and paradigmatic relationships. A noun is partly defined by the combinations into which it can enter with prefixes and suffixes. Thus we have *friendless, friendly, friendliness, unfriendly, befriend, unbefriended, friendship, unfriendliness,* but not **disfriend, *friender, *friendation, *subfriend, *overfriend, *defriendize.* The combinatory possibilities represent syntagmatic relationships, and the paradigmatic relationships are to be found in the contrast between a given morpheme and those that could replace it in a given environment. Thus, there is paradigmatic contrast between *-ly, -less,* and *-ship* in that they can all occur after *friend,* and replacement of one by another brings a change in meaning. Similarly, *friend* has paradigmatic relations with *lecture, member, dictator, partner, professor,* and so on, in that they all contrast with one another in the environment ____*ship.*

If we move up to the level of syntax proper, we can continue to identify the same types of relationship. The syntagmatic relations that define the constituent *he frightened* permit it to be followed by certain types of constituent only: *George, the man standing on the corner, thirty-one fieldmice,* etc.; but not *the stone, sincerity, purple, in,* etc. Our knowledge of syntagmatic relations enables us to define for *he frightened* a paradigmatic class of items that can follow it. These items are in paradigmatic contrast with one another, and to choose one is to produce meaning by excluding others.

Saussure claims that the entire linguistic system can be reduced to and explained in terms of a theory of syntagmatic and paradigmatic relations, and that in this sense all synchronic facts are fundamentally identical. This is perhaps the clearest assertion of what may be called the structuralist view of language: not simply that a language is a system of elements that are wholly defined by their relations to one another within the system, though it is that, but that the linguistic system consists of different levels of structure; at each level one can identify elements that contrast with one another and combine with other elements to form higher-level units, and the principles of structure at each level are fundamentally the same.

We can summarize and illustrate this view by saying that since language is form and not substance, its elements have only contrastive and combinatorial properties, and that at each level of structure one identifies the units or elements of a language by their capacity to differentiate units of the level immediately above them. We identify phonological distinctive features as the relational features that differentiate phonemes: /b/ is to /p/ and /d/ is to /t/ as voiced is to voiceless; thus voiced versus voiceless is a minimal distinctive feature. These phonemes in turn are identifiable because the contrasts between them have the capacity to differentiate morphemes: we know that /b/ and /p/ must be linguistic units because they contrast to distinguish *bet* from *pet*. And we must treat *bet* and *pet* as morphological units because the contrast between them is what differentiates, for example, *betting* from *petting* or *bets* from *pets*. Finally, these items, which we can informally call words, are defined by the fact that they play different roles in the higher-level units of phrases and sentences.

In thus asserting the mutual dependence of the various levels of language we are once again showing how it is that in linguistics nothing is given in advance. Not only that: we are arguing that one cannot first identify the elements or units of one level and then work out the way they combine to form units of the next level, because the elements with which one tries to start are defined by both syntagmatic and paradigmatic relations. The only way we can identify the prefix *re-* as a morphemic unit of English is by asking not just whether it contrasts with other elements but whether, when it combines with other elements to form a higher-level unit, it enters into contrasts which distinguish and define this higher-level combination. We know that *re-* contrasts paradigmatically with *un-, out-,* and *over-* because *redo* contrasts with *undo, outdo,* and *overdo*; and we know that *do* is a separable morphemic element because *redo* contrasts with *rebuild, reuse, reconnect*. It is, shall we say, only contrasts between words which enable us to define the lower-level constituents of words, morphemes. One must simultaneously work out syntagmatic and paradigmatic relations. This basic structural principle, that items are defined by their contrasts with other items and their ability to combine to form higher-level items, operates at every level of language.

Language as Social Fact

In explaining these technical aspects of Saussure's theory of language I have not emphasized sufficiently one principle to which he gave great weight: that in analyzing a language we are analyzing social facts, dealing with the social use of material objects. As I have said, a language could be realized in various substances without alteration to its basic nature as a system of relations. What is important, indeed all that is relevant, are the distinctions and relations that have been endowed with meaning by a society. The question the analyst constantly asks is what are the differences that have meaning for members of the speech community. It may often be difficult to assign a precise form to those things that function as signs, but if a difference bears meaning for members of a culture, then there is a sign, however abstract, which must be analyzed. For speakers of English, *John loves Mary* is different in meaning from *Mary loves John;* therefore the word-order constitutes a sign, a social fact, whereas some physical differences between the way two speakers utter the sentence *John loves Mary* may bear no meaning and therefore be purely material facts, not social facts.

We can see then that linguistics studies not large collections of sound sequences but a system of social conventions. One is trying to determine the units and rules of combination which make up that system and which make possible linguistic communication between members of a society. It is one of the virtues of Saussure's theory of language to have placed social conventions and social facts at the center of linguistic investigation by stressing the problem of the sign. What are the signs of this linguistic system? On what does their identity as signs depend? Asking these simple questions, demonstrating that nothing can be taken for granted as a unit of language, Saussure continually stressed the importance of adopting the right methodological perspective and seeing language as a system of socially determined values, not as a collection of substantially defined elements. One might, to conclude this discussion, quote two relevant passages which he actually wrote:

The ultimate law of language is, dare we say, that nothing can ever reside in a single term. This is a direct consequence of the fact that linguistic signs are unrelated to what they designate, and that therefore *a* cannot designate anything without the aid of *b* and vice versa, or, in other words, that both have value only by the differences between them, or that neither has value, in any of its constituents, except through this same network of forever negative differences.

Since language consists of no substance but only of the isolated or combined action of physiological, psychological, and mental forces; and since nevertheless of all our distinctions, our whole terminology, all our ways of speaking about it are molded by the involuntary assumption that there is substance, one cannot avoid recognizing, before all else, that the most essential task of linguistic theory will be to disentangle the state of our basic distinctions. I cannot grant anyone the right to construct a theory while avoiding the work of definition, although this convenient procedure seems so far to have satisfied students of language.[3]

To promote dissatisfaction and stimulate thought about fundamentals, to insist on the relational nature of linguistic phenomena: these are the vectors of Saussure's theory. We can now consider the wider significance of his work: its relation to previous and subsequent thought about language, and to work in other disciplines.

[3]"Notes inédites de F. de Saussure," *Cahiers Ferdinand de Saussure* 12 (1954), 63 and 55–56.

3

The Place of Saussure's Theories

There are three different contexts in which one can attempt
to assess the significance of Saussure's thought, and although
this may involve a bit of repetition in setting out the importance of particular concepts or insights, it seems best to consider, in turn, Saussure's relation to his predecessors in linguistics, the relations between Saussure's theories of language
and major currents of thought outside linguistics, and, finally, Saussure's influence on modern linguistics and the for-
tune of his ideas among his successors. This broad panorama
is necessary because the importance of Saussure lies not simply in his contribution to linguistics per se but in the way he
made what might otherwise have seemed a recondite and specialized discipline a major intellectual presence and model for
other disciplines of the "human sciences." In other words, the
implicit claim of this chapter is that in looking at the way
Saussure responded to the state of linguistics in his day and at
the theoretical basis on which he proposed to renovate linguistics, we shall discover fundamental insights about the
study of human behavior and social objects.

Linguistics before Saussure

The *Course in General Linguistics* begins with a compressed
version of Saussure's remarks on the history of linguistics.

Setting aside the study of language prior to 1800, he distinguishes two stages of linguistic investigation: that of comparative philology or comparative grammar, which dates from Franz Bopp's work of 1816 (it compared the conjugation system of Sanskrit with that of other languages), and a second period, beginning roughly in 1870, when comparative philology became more properly historical and when some linguists began asking pertinent questions about the nature of language and linguistic method.

Of linguistics before 1800 Saussure has very little to say, probably because he was much less concerned with general problems of intellectual history than with methods of linguistic analysis and the definition of linguistic facts. But if we are thinking about the wider significance of Saussure's own theory, we cannot avoid considering how far Saussure's revolt against the linguistics of his own century involved a dialectical working out of some of the underlying principles or implications of linguistic study prior to the nineteenth century. My account will necessarily be sketchy, selective, and abstract, but it is essential if we are to see what Saussure rediscovered or preserved of previous thought about language.

People choosing to devote themselves to the study of language assume that they are undertaking something worthwhile, and although they may not necessarily have formulated a view about the purpose of studying language, the assumptions on which their work is based will necessarily shape their discipline. An age which assumes, for example, that linguistics will give insight into the characteristics of the nation or race will produce a very different discipline from one which assumes that linguistics will cast light on the nature of human thought and of the mind itself.

This latter assumption structured and animated the study of language in the seventeenth and eighteenth centuries: by studying language one sought to understand thought itself. But the study of language takes two different forms, according to the type of question asked about thought. The first approach, which is essentially of the seventeenth century and is best represented by the Port Royal Grammar (*Grammaire générale et raisonnée*), takes language as a picture or an image of thought and therefore seeks through a study of language to discover a universal logic, the laws of reason. The main enterprise is a rational explanation of the parts of speech and grammatical categories. Thus we are told, for example, that the verb is essentially a representation of affirmation, so that the true universal verb is *to be.* Languages have, however, joined in their verbs the truly verbal function of affirmation or predication and the other nonverbal function of designating an attribute. *Peter lives* is analyzed in logical grammar as *Peter is living,* where the true verb, *is,* predicates the attribute *living* of Peter.

Grammar of this kind was wholly atemporal or synchronic. Saussure himself, asking rather insultingly "how did those who studied language before the foundation of linguistic proceed?" noted that the seventeenth-century grammarians' point of view was "irreproachable." They had a well-defined object, knew what they were doing, and did not confuse synchronic and diachronic studies, though their practice was wanting in many other respects (*Course,* 82; *Cours,* 118). But it was precisely this absence of a temporal dimension that worried their eighteenth-century successors. If one wishes to understand thought, they suggested, it is not enough to work out a logical grammar; one must discuss the formation or development of ideas. For followers of Locke this was especially crucial: to understand the human mind one must know how ideas are developed from sensations, and it was precisely this problem which Condillac, the eighteenth-century *savant* and linguist, addressed in his *Essay on the Origin of Human Knowledge.*

Condillac set out to demonstrate that reflection can be derived from sensation and that the mechanism of derivation is a "linking of ideas" brought about through the use of signs. The precise nature of his argument is not important; what is important is the direction in which it leads him. Trying to show that thought has a natural origin, that the existence of reflection and abstract notions is something that can be explained, he went beyond the claim that language is a picture of thought (the seventeenth-century position) to argue that abstract ideas are a result of the process by which signs are created. He had therefore to demonstrate that there was a natural process by which a language of conventional signs could arise from a primitive and nonreflective experience. He had to concern himself with the origin of language.

Through Condillac and his followers the origin of language became a central problem of eighteenth-century thought; but it is essential to note that it was investigated as a philosophical rather than a historical problem. One worked on the origin of language in order to shed light on the nature of language and thus on the nature of thought. By explaining the origin of something, one explained its nature. And thus eighteenth-century thinking about language came to focus especially on what one might call philosophic etymology: the attempt to explain signs and abstract ideas by imagining their origins in gesture, action, and sensation. Condillac suggests, for example, that prepositions were originally the names of gestures indicating direction. The reason for such hypotheses is perhaps amply indicated in Locke's suggestion, taken up at length in Turgot's article on etymology in the *Encyclopédie,* that study of the origins of words would indicate the concepts which Nature itself has suggested to men.

The desire to study in language the mechanism of the mind led to a search for primitive roots: the essential elements which, with their meaning, lie at the core of all signs that have since developed from them. A root was a rudimentary name, a basic representation, and later developments could be thought of as metaphorical extensions or accretions, if not distortions, of these basic signs. The derivations in Horne Tooke's *The Diversions of Purley* are only the most amusing examples of a mode of thought extremely common in England and France in the eighteenth century.

Here is Tooke on the root *bar*:

> A *bar* in all its uses is a *defence*: that by which anything is fortified, strengthened or defended. A *barn* is a covered enclosure in which the grain, etc. is protected or defended from the weather, from depredations, etc. A *baron* is an armed, defenceful, or powerful man. A *barge* is a strong boat. A *bargain* is a confirmed, strengthened agreement.... A *bark* is a stout vessel. The *bark* of a tree is its defence....

This, as I say, is an extreme example, but it illustrates several important points. First of all, the study of language is founded on a notion of representation; it is because words are taken as signs which represent fundamental categories of experience that they are of interest, and it is according to these categories that they are grouped. Unity of representation or meaning is what is used to bring these words together.

Second, in order to cast light on thought, the analyst attempts to motivate signs: *baron* is not simply the arbitrary combination of a phonological sequence and a meaning; it is motivated by its supposed derivation from a primitive root which is in itself the natural basis of all related signs. In general, the etymological project assumes that the words of our language are not arbitrary signs but have a rational basis and are motivated by resemblance to a primitive sign.

Third, time is here invoked, as so often in the eighteenth century, not in the interests of any historical project but as an explanatory fiction. This of course opened the way for a more accurate historical study of linguistic evolution which, by destroying philosophic etymologies, was to strike at the heart of the philosophic project. In invoking history, albeit as a fiction, eighteenth-century students of language made themselves especially vulnerable.

Finally, the relationship between language and mind is conceived atomistically. It is when they are taken individually, or in individual groups, that signs illustrate the nature of the mind and mental operations. The connection between language and mind is here being made not through the logical structures of seventeenth-century philosophic grammar nor through the concept of *a language* or linguistic system, which Saussure would emphasize, but through natural concepts represented by individual roots.

Nineteenth-century linguistics would reject these four concerns or procedures. As Hans Aarsleff argues:

> It is universally agreed that the decisive turn in language study occurred when the philosophical, a priori method of the eighteenth century was abandoned in favor of the historical, a posteriori method of the nineteenth. The former began with mental categories and sought their exemplification in language, as in universal grammar, and based etymologies on conjectures about the origin of language. The latter sought only facts, evidence, demonstration; it divorced the study of language from the study of mind.[1]

Rejecting the link between language and mind, the nineteenth century lost interest in the word as a sign or representation. The word became a form which was to be compared with other forms so as to establish the relations between languages, or else a form whose historical evolution was to be traced. The fictional history of the philosophic etymologies

[1]*The Study of Language in England, 1780–1860* (Princeton: Princeton University Press, 1967), p. 127. This is an excellent discussion of the history of linguistics, with a wider scope than its title indicates.

was abandoned for a properly positivistic history, and with it was abandoned the attempt to use history to motivate signs. The object of study for nineteenth-century linguistics, in short, was no longer the sign as a representation whose rational basis must be discovered, but the form whose resemblances and historical links with other forms must be demonstrated.

Though linguists generally see nineteenth-century developments as a great advance, something was obviously lost in this shift in interest; and when Saussure came to take issue with his immediate predecessors, he returned, albeit at a different level of sophistication and in a different way, to the concerns of the eighteenth century. First of all, he returned to the problem of the sign and once again conceived of language as an order of representation. He saw that unless one treats linguistic forms as signs, one cannot define them; but by placing the problem of the sign in the context of his methodological inquiry he avoided the atomism of his eighteenth-century predecessors: signs are constituted only by their relations with other signs, so the project of studying individual signs as representations must be abandoned. Moreover, Saussure re-establishes, at least implicitly, the relationship between the study of language and the study of mind, but once again at another level and in a different methodological context. What the study of language reveals about mind is not a set of primitive conceptions or natural ideas but the general structuring and differentiating operations by which things are made to signify. When Saussure argues that meaning is "diacritical" or differential, based on differences between terms and not on intrinsic properties of terms themselves, his claim concerns not only language but the general human process in which the mind creates meaning by distinguishing.

One might say, summarizing very briefly, that eighteenth-century linguistics was an example of misplaced concreteness. The link between language and thought was made in too direct, too concrete a fashion: through individual signs whose autonomy was assumed. In order to come back to the problem in a different perspective, in order to see that it was the general mechanisms of language as a semiotic system that illustrate the properties of mind, the link between language and mind had to be broken for a time and language had to be studied as an object in itself. It had to be treated, temporarily, as a system of forms with no special relation to mind. This was the role of nineteenth-century linguistics.

In discussing the development of "comparative grammar" or comparative philology in the nineteenth century, Saussure notes that it might not have taken place, at least not so swiftly, without Europe's discovery of Sanskrit. English rule in India and the interest taken in Indian languages by English administrators brought to the attention of European linguists the surprising affinities between Sanskrit and early European languages, such as Greek and Latin. These relationships between verbal roots and between grammatical forms seemed to late eighteenth-century linguists too numerous to be fortuitous and led them to postulate a common source for the three languages.

Sanskrit encouraged the comparison of languages because, as Saussure shows, it not only possessed affinities with other Indo-European languages but helped to make clear the relations between those languages themselves. Consider the declensions of these nouns:

Latin:	genus	generis	genere	genera	generum
Greek:	génos	géneos	génei	génea	géneōn
Sanskrit:	ǵanas	ǵanasas	ǵanasi	ǵanassu	ǵanasām

If the Latin and Greek alone are compared with one another, there does not seem to be much direct affinity; but when the Sanskrit is added it helps to suggest the nature of the relationship between them: where the Sanskrit has an *s* between two vowels, the Latin has an *r* while the Greek has no consonant. There are still, of course, considerable differences between the vowels, but the comparison of these grammatical forms—the inflectional endings of nouns—certainly suggests strong affinities.

With the emergence of this new and revealing data, the task of linguistics became comparison, but not the comparison of isolated forms that had so intrigued eighteenth-century linguists. The aim was to find patterns of affinity, not to discover a primitive meaning or representation which a root like *bar* might bear in all its manifestations. And so emphasis fell on inflectional systems—precisely the elements which philosophic etymologists stripped away to get at the roots, or else treated as detachable elements that were themselves derived from other roots. Friedrich von Schlegel, in *On the Language and Wisdom of the Indians* (1808), conceded the existence of common roots, but argued that "the decisive point, however, which will clarify everything here, is the inner structure of the languages or comparative grammar, which will give us entirely new information about the genealogy of language in the same way as comparative anatomy has shed light upon natural history."

It was, as I suggested above, necessary to break the connection between the study of language and the study of mind in order to approach a better understanding of language as a system. The shift of attention from roots to inflectional patterns (which had always been the most difficult items for philosophic etymologists to deal with) reflects a change in the notion of what language is: no longer is it simply a representation, a series of forms ordered by the rationality they represent and through which one moves to grasp thought and the processes of mind itself; it is a system of forms that are governed by their own law, that possess an autonomous formal pattern. The idea of comparing languages, not in terms of the

73

roots which they use to express the fundamental concepts or categories of experience, but in terms of the formal patterns of grammatical elements through which words are linked and differentiated, is a major step toward the notion of a language as a formal and autonomous system.

Indeed, as Schlegel suggested in the sentence quoted above, language was now conceived as an object of knowledge, something which could be dissected or anatomized like a plant or an animal. No longer was it being studied as the form of thought itself, as a representation of the mind's relation to the world. Michel Foucault notes:

> From the nineteenth century language began to fold in upon itself, to acquire its own particular density, to deploy a history, an objectivity, and laws of its own. It became one object of knowledge among others, on the same level as living beings, wealth and value, and the history of events and man. . . . To know language is no longer to come as close as possible to knowledge itself; it is merely to apply the methods of understanding in general to a particular domain of objectivity.[2]

The method was that of comparison; the goal was the demonstration of affinities; and the fundamental methodological principle was that analogies between inflectional systems were the criterion of linguistic relationship. But comparative study had striking results. It led to the formulation of what were called "sound laws": general rules or tables of correspondence which stated that a particular set of sounds in one language corresponded to another set of sounds in another language. The most famous of these is Grimm's law, named after Jacob Grimm, who, with Bopp, Schlegel, and Rasmus Rask, was one of the foremost comparative grammarians.

[2]*The Order of Things* (New York: Pantheon, 1971), p. 296.

Grimm's law is actually a series of nine correspondences: Germanic languages have a *t* where Latin, Greek, and Sanskrit have a *d*; an *f* where they have a *p* (these two correspondences are illustrated by words for "foot": early Germanic *fotus,* as opposed to Greek *podos,* Latin *pedes,* and Sanskrit *padas*); Germanic has a *b* where Latin has an *f,* Greek a *ph,* and Sanskrit a *bh*; and so on, for six other correspondences.

Saussure says that these comparative grammarians never succeeded in founding a true linguistics because they did not try to determine the nature of the object they were studying and did not ask what was the significance of the relationships they discovered (*Course,* 3; *Cours,* 16). Their method was exclusively comparative rather than historical. They spoke as if there were an abstract universal pattern, a series of slots which each language had to fill with some elements, and they thus confused the synchronic and diachronic perspectives. In fact, the parallels they discovered between languages indicated a historical relationship, and the diachronic task would be to reconstruct in detail the steps by which elements of an original Indo-European language became the elements of Sanskrit, Greek, Latin, and so on. The synchronic task, on the other hand, would be to show how, at a particular stage in the development of a language, the fortuitously given historical elements were organized into a system peculiar to that language.

The confusion of these two tasks, says Saussure, can be seen in Grimm, who is not a proper historical linguist. He fails to distinguish diachronic changes from the synchronic function given to new elements by the linguistic system. We saw in the previous chapter (p. 54) that vowel alternation, as in *foot*: *feet, goose*: *geese, tooth*: *teeth,* was the result of a purely phonetic change that did not concern grammar. But Grimm sees vowel alternation as naturally significant in itself: the vowel of *foot* becomes the vowel of *feet* in order to represent the plural (Engler, 15). It is as if a role had to be filled and the language had grown or developed a new part in order to fill it. Saussure thought this kind of plausible but woolly thinking most insidious.

There was, of course, a reason for this kind of thinking, a prestigious model to which linguists were implicitly appealing. This was the model of the living organism: a self-contained entity that grew and developed according to general laws. As we have seen, Schlegel related comparative grammar to comparative anatomy, and the metaphor is not uncommon in linguistic writings. Comparative anatomy, presiding over the transformation by which natural history became biology, directed research toward the inner organic structure of living beings. Plants or animals could then be related to one another in terms of the different ways in which their organisms fulfilled basic functions, such as respiration, reproduction, digestion, locomotion, circulation. These relations, in turn, led to the production of historical taxonomies: evolutionary schemes in which the notion of history could be used to bring together and explain the differences between the organic system of each species, as revealed by comparison.

The common ground between linguistics and biology in the early nineteenth century is this: both were engaged in breaking away from the fictional historical continuity which animated eighteenth-century research. The only way to do proper history was to break with history in the first instance, to treat individual languages or species as autonomous entities that could be described and compared with one another as wholes. Then, given these individual organisms, it became possible to rediscover history but at a new level. Once the living being has been analyzed as an organism which finds ways of fulfilling basic functions, it has been analyzed in terms of the conditions which enable it to have a history. That is to say, the history of the organism or of the species becomes the story of the way in which these basic functions are fulfilled, the story of the changes which it undergoes in order to maintain its existence. The elementary functions become the basis of a historical series. Thus, the ahistorical work of comparative anatomy is what made Darwin's theory of evolution possible.

Similarly, in the case of language the comparative method breaks with philosophic etymology in order to consider languages as comparable systems. Comparison shows the different ways in which languages fulfill similar functions (e.g., the different inflectional systems for nouns). The analogies between these differences then call for historical explanation, for the postulation of an evolutionary tree. But here linguistics seems to have taken Lamarckian rather than Darwinian evolutionary theory as a model, with the result that languages were conceived of as evolving in a purposeful way, deliberately adapting to changes. There was a confusion between the synchronic facts—the use to which changed forms were put by the grammatical system—and diachronic facts, the sound changes themselves.

But to state the comparison in this way, as if biology were a bad influence, is no doubt unfair to biology, for Darwin himself stated quite plainly the principle which Saussure saw as essential to a proper understanding of linguistics. Any purposiveness in biological evolution, Darwin saw, does not lie in changes themselves but wholly in the process of natural selection, which is, in a sense, a synchronic process. New species develop from accidental or random mutations, which themselves have no direction or purpose. But some mutants fare better than others in the ecological system of a particular moment. The failures die, the successes persist within the system, and thus a change in the species has been brought about. But mutations, like vowel changes, do not occur *in order* to bring about a better adapted species. Change in the species is a use to which the system puts mutations. It is a result of mutation but, like synchronic facts, is not the goal or purpose of the original event.

77

Ferdinand de Saussure

The Neogrammarians

It was only toward 1870, Saussure wrote, that linguists began to lay the foundation for a proper study of language. There were two important developments in which Saussure himself played a significant role. First, a group of linguists now known as the Neogrammarians, and among whom were Saussure's teachers at Leipzig, demonstrated that sound laws, which previously had been treated as correspondences that held in large numbers of cases but not in others, operated *without exception*. As Herman Osthoff and Karl Brugmann wrote, "every sound change, in as much as it occurs mechanically, takes place according to laws that admit no exception. That is, the direction of the sound shift is always the same for all members of the linguistic community, except where a split into dialects occurs; and all the words in which the sound subjected to the change appears in the same relationship are affected by the change without exception." The demonstration involved the discovery that sound changes were perfectly regular if one formulated in a sufficiently precise way the phonetic environments in which changes occurred (e.g., Sanskrit *t* corresponds to early Germanic *th* when it follows an accented syllable but otherwise to early Germanic *d*).

This may seem a minor technical advance, but the principle at stake—of change without exceptions—is crucial, for reasons which perhaps none but Saussure understood. The absolute nature of sound change is a consequence of the arbitrary nature of the sign. Since the sign is arbitrary, there is no reason for a change in sound not to apply to all instances of that sound; whereas if sounds were motivated ("naturally" expressive, like *bow-wow*), then there would be resistance, depending on the degree of motivation, and exceptions. There are no exceptions because, given the arbitrary nature of the sound and its phonetic realizations, change does not apply directly to signs themselves but to sounds, or, rather, to a single

78

sound in a particular environment. It is as if, Saussure says, a string on a piano had been tightened or loosened: when we play a melody, there will be a lot of false notes; but it would be wrong to say that the first note in the third bar, the second note in the fourth bar, the first note in the sixth bar, and so on, had all changed. These changes are all consequences of one change in the system of realization. "The system of sounds is the instrument on which we articulate the words of our language; if one of these elements is modified, there can be diverse consequences, but the fact in itself does not concern words which are, as it were, the melodies of our repertoire" (*Course,* 94; *Cours,* 134).

The second important development after 1870, according to Saussure, was that "the results of comparative study were brought into historical sequence" and linguists tried to construct in detail the historical sequence which alone would explain the results of comparison (Engler, 17). Saussure himself made a major contribution to historical linguistics in his *Memoir* of 1878 on the Indo-European vowel system, a work which showed the fecundity of thinking of language as a system of purely relational items, even when attempting historical reconstruction.

Saussure was interested in the problem of vowel alternation in Indo-European. The question was what vowel system must the original Indo-European language have had to account for the patterns of vowel alternation found in the known languages that derive from it. The most difficult aspect of this question was the vowel *a.* Other scholars had postulated several different *a*'s in an attempt to explain the divergent results in other languages. Saussure found their solutions unsatisfactory and argued that in addition to two *a*'s, there must have been another phoneme which he could describe in formal terms: it was unrelated to *e* or *o* (which derived from the two *a*'s), it could stand alone to form a syllable, like a vowel, but it could also combine with another vowel, like a consonant. He did not try to define its substance but called it a "sonant coefficient" and treated it as a purely formal and relational unit in the vowel system. What makes Saussure's work so very impressive is that nearly fifty years later, when cuneiform Hittite was discovered and deciphered, it was found to contain a phoneme, written *h*, which behaved as Saussure had predicted. He had discovered, by a purely formal analysis, what are now known as the laryngeals of Indo-European.[3]

Saussure certainly proved himself an accomplished Neogrammarian, and on many points he admired their accomplishments. He praised them for seeing, for example, that the phenomenon known as "false analogy" to earlier linguists was not to be despised but was important in linguistic evolution, especially as a counterbalance to the effect of sound change. Consider the Latin *honor:* the original form was *honos*: *honosem* (nominative and accusative). By the sound change I have mentioned above (p. 73) an *s* between two vowels became *r*, giving *honos*: *honorem*. But since there existed other paradigms such as *orator*: *oratorem* which were now apparently "regular," a new form (*honor*) developed "by analogy" with them.

The Neogrammarians were the first to recognize how important this procedure was in restructuring languages, but even they, Saussure notes, were mistaken about its true nature and confused the synchronic and the diachronic aspects (*Course,* 163; *Cours,* 224). The production of a new form, Saussure argues, is a synchronic phenomenon, comparable with the creative exploitation of combinatory possibilities that occurs when from *market* the language creates *marketeer* on the analogy of, say, *profiteer*. For Saussure, one may recall, there is no difference in kind between morphological and syntactic combinations, so that this sort of new forma-

[3]The *Mémoire* and other highly technical papers can be found in the *Recueil des publications scientifiques de F. de Saussure* (Geneva, 1922).

tion is comparable to the production of a new sentence and not an example of significant change in the language. What happens in the case we are considering is that the new form and the old form, *honor* and *honos,* continue to exist side by side as optional variants, and when eventually the old form disappears, this is not a significant change but only the elimination of a variant realization. The Neogrammarians gave too much weight to the historical perspective and failed to recognize the systematic and grammatical (i.e., fundamentally synchronic) nature of the phenomena they were studying.

But the real fault of Saussure's contemporaries was that they failed to ask themselves fundamental questions about what they were studying: questions about the nature of language itself and its individual forms, and important methodological questions about identity in linguistics, both synchronic and diachronic. The Neogrammarians could not do this because they had abandoned representation as the basis of their discipline: they were not thinking about signs, and for Saussure, as we have seen, only by thinking about signs and their nature could one begin to discriminate between the functional and the nonfunctional aspects of language and attain an appropriately relational concept of linguistic units.

The Neogrammarians were concerned not with signs but with forms. If one asks under what conditions linguistic forms could become an object of knowledge, become the material of a discipline, one reaches the heart of the Neogrammarian position. Earlier comparative linguists such as Bopp had clung to meaning and representation, not as what linguistics was attempting to analyze (as had been the case for eighteenth-century philosophic etymologists) but as the condition of comparison: one looked at the words which various languages used to express a particular concept and thus used continuity of meaning as a way of bringing forms together and justifying comparison. But as soon as linguists asked what was the significance of these comparisons, they were led to try to found their discipline on a historical continuity. If similarities in form were not fortuitous, they indicated common origin, and the task became that of postulating original forms and following the historical evolution that linked original forms with later forms in an unbroken series. Whence the appositeness of biological metaphors, one of whose consequences is to exclude questions of representation. A plant does not stand for something; it is not the bearer of a meaning: it is a form that grows according to laws which must be discovered.

In fact, the Neogrammarians had abandoned the biological metaphors, which belonged to the mid-nineteenth century; but in rejecting these metaphors as essentially mystical they retained two of their corollaries: the neglect of questions of representation and the assumption that their science must be based on historical continuity and must analyze historical evolution. Saussure was suspicious of notions of historical continuity, and he saw that study of the historical evolution of forms could easily lead to misunderstanding and neglect of questions of linguistic function. The diachronic perspective prevents one from asking the questions which would lead to pertinent synchronic description. And so it was for him a major development when the American linguist William Dwight Whitney, working within what was still essentially the Neogrammarian tradition, began to raise the question of the sign. In his books *Language and the Study of Language* (1867) and *The Life and Growth of Language* (1875), Whitney had argued that "language is, in fact, an institution," founded on social convention, "a body of usages prevailing in a certain community," a "treasure of words and forms," each of which "is an arbitrary and conventional sign." In thus stressing the institutional and conventional nature of language, Saussure says, "he placed linguistics on its true axis" (*Course*, 76; *Cours*, 110). But Whitney did not realize the consequences and implications of this new perspective. He still asserted that linguistics must be a historical science: its task to seek causes, to explain why we speak as we do. He vastly underestimated the task of synchronic linguistics, writing that "a mere apprehension and exposition of the phenomena of a language—of its words, its forms, its rules, its usages: that is work for grammarians and lexicographers." He thus demonstrated that he had no awareness of problems of definition and identity, of the relational nature of linguistic units, and little interest generally in the questions concerning foundations that obsessed Saussure.

More important, perhaps, for Saussure, was the example of Hippolyte Taine, a leading intellectual figure in late nineteenth century France, whose widely read *De l'intelligence* focused on signs as what make the world perceptible and intelligible. First published in 1870 and regularly reprinted during Saussure's lifetime, *De l'intelligence* contains, Hans Aarsleff contends, "all the elements of Saussure's doctrine of signs," even the analogy, which Saussure uses, that physical event and mental event are correlated "like the recto and verso of a surface."[4] Taine also revived the legacy of Condillac and thus helped inspire Saussure to return to the problem of the sign and see that it was only by once again making representation rather than history the basis of a discipline that one could begin to distinguish the relevant from the irrelevant, the functional from the nonfunctional.

Saussure returned to representation, but he conceived it and employed it in a different way. Linguistics would no longer be founded on continuity of representation (a common essential meaning for a whole series of forms), as it had been for the philosophic etymologists; on the contrary, discontinuity would be the ground of representation. Meanings

[4]Aarsleff, "Taine and Saussure," *From Locke to Saussure: Essays on the Study of Language and Intellectual History* (Minneapolis: University of Minnesota Press, 1982), p. 358 and pp. 356–71 passim.

exist only because there are differences of meaning, and it is these differences of meaning that enable one to establish the articulation of forms. Forms can be recognized not by their persistence in a representational or historical continuity but by their differential function within a language: their ability to distinguish and thus produce distinct meanings.

This fundamental perception is made possible by Saussure's realization that questions about what *a language* is are more basic than questions about what language is. The eighteenth and nineteenth centuries had both focused not on a language but on language, either as the medium of thought or as an evolving series of forms. Saussure saw that any understanding of what language is required a prior understanding of what a language is (hence his insistence that linguistics focus on *la langue*, the system of a language). The idea of a language as a system of forms defined by their relations to one another is implicit in monolingual dictionaries, which had existed since the seventeenth century, but it had never been given a central place in systematic discussion of language.[5]

By granting priority to questions about a language, and thus focusing on the system of linguistic forms, Saussure achieved an insight of revolutionary significance, not to be found in Whitney or his other predecessors: meaning depends on difference of meaning within a system; only through difference of meaning can one identify forms and their defining functional qualities. Forms are not given but must be established through analysis of a system of relations and differences. This notion, as we shall see in Chapter 4, makes possi-

[5]Roy Harris makes this point in his brilliant book *The Language Makers* (Ithaca: Cornell University Press, 1980), pp. 29–30 and 127–36. The Saussurian concept of a synchronic language system, he suggests, has as its basis "the contents of an idealised non-historical monolingual dictionary" (p. 155). The dictionary had become "so firmly established as an authoritative guide to linguistic usage" that when a linguistic theory reflecting its conception of a language eventually appeared, "it was immediately accepted as capturing a fundamental truth about languages" (p. 149).

ble a way of studying human behavior and objects that is only today coming into its own. In reinstating representation but focusing on its discontinuities, Saussure helped to lay the foundations of modern thought.

Freud, Durkheim, and Method

In order to understand more clearly Saussure's modernity we might abandon linguistics for a moment and place the founder of modern linguistics with his two exact contemporaries: Sigmund Freud, the founder of modern psychology, and Emile Durkheim, the founder of modern sociology. These three thinkers revolutionized the social sciences by creating for their work a new epistemological context: that is to say, they conceived of their objects of study in a different way and offered a new mode of explanation.

The initial problem for a social science is the nature and status of the facts with which it is dealing. This was a particularly acute problem in the late nineteenth century because the two principal strains of the period's philosophical heritage, German idealism and an empiricist positivism, met at one point: their tendency to think of society as a result, a secondary or derived phenomenon, rather than something primary. The positivists, in a Humean tradition, distinguished between an objective physical reality of objects and events and an individual subjective perception of reality. Society could not qualify as the former and thus came to be treated as the result of feelings and actions of individuals. As Jeremy Bentham wrote, "society is a fictitious body, the sum of the several members who compose it." Indeed, the assumption that society is the result of individuals, each acting in accordance with self-interest, is the very basis of utilitarianism. And Durkheim, criticizing his predecessors, wrote that for them, "there is nothing real in society except the individual. . . . The individual is the sole tangible reality that the observer can attain." For Hegel, on the other hand, laws, manners, customs, and the state itself are expressions of Mind as it evolves and are thus to be studied as manifestations or results, not as primary phenomena. Neither view is especially propitious to the development of social sciences.

Saussure, Durkheim, and Freud seem to have recognized that this view gets things the wrong way around. For human beings, society is a primary reality, not just the sum of individual activities, nor the contingent manifestations of Mind; and if one wishes to study human behavior, one must grant that there is a social reality. People live not simply among objects and actions but among objects and actions that have meaning, and these meanings cannot be treated as a sum of subjective perceptions. They are the very furniture of the world. The social significance of actions, the meanings of utterances, feelings of love, anger, guilt, and so forth, cannot be lightly dismissed. They are social facts. As Durkheim repeatedly stated, and his two contemporaries would have agreed, his discipline is based on the "objective reality of social facts."

In short, sociology, linguistics, and psychoanalytic psychology are possible only when one takes the meanings which are attached to and which differentiate objects and actions in society as a primary reality, as facts to be explained. And since meanings are a social product, explanation must be carried out in social terms. It is as if Saussure, Freud, and Durkheim had asked, "What makes individual experience possible? What enables men and women to operate with meaningful objects and actions? What enables them to communicate and act meaningfully?" And the answer they postulated was social institutions which, though formed by human activities, are the conditions of experience. To understand individual experience one must study the social norms which make it possible.

It is not difficult to see why this should be so. When two people meet they may act politely or impolitely, and the politeness or impoliteness of their behavior is a social and cultural fact. But an objective description of the physical actions they perform would not be a description of a social phenomenon because it would leave out of account the social conventions which make the actions what they are. Their behavior is meaningful only with respect to a set of social conventions: it is these conventions that make it possible to be polite or impolite; they create behavior which must therefore be described in their terms. Similarly, making a noise is not in itself a social phenomenon, but uttering a sentence is. The social phenomenon is made possible by a system of interpersonal conventions: a language.

Saussure, Freud, and Durkheim thus reverse the perspective which makes society the result of individual behavior and insist that behavior is made possible by collective social systems individuals have assimilated, consciously or unconsciously. It was Freud, Lionel Trilling wrote, who "made it apparent to us how entirely implicated in culture we all are . . . how the culture suffuses the remotest parts of the individual mind," making possible a whole series of feelings and actions and even the individual's sense of identity. Individual actions and symptoms can be interpreted psychoanalytically because they are the result of common psychic processes, unconscious defenses occasioned by social taboos and leading to particular types of repression and displacement. Linguistic communication is possible because we have assimilated a system of collective norms that organize the world and give meaning to verbal acts. Or again, as Durkheim argued, the reality crucial to the individual is not the physical environment but the social milieu, a system of rules and norms, of collective representations, which makes possible social behavior.

This perspective therefore involves a special type of expla-

nation: to explain an action is to relate it to the underlying
system of norms which makes it possible. The action is explained as a manifestation of an underlying system of representations. Whether this is still to be regarded as causal explanation varies from one case to another. In his work on
suicide, perhaps his most famous sociological investigation,
Durkheim claimed to offer a causal explanation; but he was
identifying the causes of high suicide rates in a society, not
explaining why particular individuals commit suicide at a
given moment. Their suicides are manifestations of the weak-
ening in social bonds that results from a particular configuration of social norms. Freud's psychological analyses are usually presented as causal explanations, but they do not have
predictive force (he is not claiming that a given sequence of
events will necessarily produce certain actions or symptoms)
and are perhaps best regarded as an attempt to relate actions
to an underlying psychic economy. Linguistics, on the other
hand, does not pretend to causal analysis: it does not try
to explain why an individual uttered a particular sequence
at a given moment, but it shows why the sequence has the
form and meaning it does by relating it to the system of the
language.

In each case, then, despite pretensions to causal analysis,
one might say that what is being offered is a structural rather
than a causal explanation: one attempts to show why a particular action has significance by relating it to the system of
underlying functions, norms, and categories which make it
possible.

What is especially significant in this reorientation is the
move away from historical explanation. To explain social
phenomena is not to discover temporal antecedents and to
link them in a causal chain, but to specify the place and function of phenomena in a system. There is a move from the
diachronic to the synchronic perspective, which one might
speak of as an internalizing of causation: instead of conceiv-

88

ing of causation on a historical model, where temporal development makes something what it is, the historical results are detemporalized and treated simply as a state, a condition.

This is a complex but fundamental displacement, which we have already seen at work in Saussure's insistence that actual historical change which produces forms such as *foot* and *feet* is not an important explanatory factor in our analysis of a language. What is important is the state, in which the distinction between singular and plural is marked by a difference in vowels. The presence of this vocalic opposition in the system is a result of a historical process, but it is the system's use of that opposition which has explanatory value.

But the most striking example of this displacement, this internalization of causality, is to be found in Freud's work on the Oedipus complex, where we have the spectacle of a mind still attracted to historical and causal explanation while at least partially aware that this is not what his new mode of analysis requires. In *Totem and Taboo* (1918), discussing the prohibition of incest and other social taboos, Freud postulates a historical event in primitive times: a jealous and tyrannical father, who wished to keep all the women for himself and drove away his sons as they reached maturity, was killed and devoured by the sons who had banded together. In devouring him, they sought to take on his power and his role. This "memorable and criminal deed" was the beginning of "social organization, of moral restrictions, and of religion," because guilt and remorse created taboos. Freud recognizes that in making this deed the historical cause of social norms and psychic complexes that still exist, he is postulating the continuity of a collective psyche, which he calls the unconscious. How otherwise could a single act continue to exercise such profound effects on humanity? Part of the explanation, Freud says, is that in our psychic economy feelings of guilt may arise from wishes as well as from actual deeds, and "this creative sense of guilt" helps to keep the consequences of the deed alive. Indeed, he admits it is possible that the original deed never actually took place; remorse may have been provoked by the sons' fantasy of killing the father. This is a plausible hypothesis, he says, and "no damage would thus be done to the causal chain stretching from the beginning to the present day." In fact, the question of whether the deed really took place or not "does not in our judgment affect the heart of the matter." But primitive men were uninhibited. For them "thought passes directly into action. And that is why, without laying claim to any finality of judgment, I think that in the case before us it may be safely assumed that 'in the beginning was the Deed.'"

Freud here appears very much in the guise of an eighteenth-century thinker, using fictions of origin to discuss the nature of a thing. What is most important, however, is his recognition that if the original deed is to serve as a true historical cause, one must postulate an underlying psychic system which, in turn, makes the deed itself unnecessary. The guilt resulting from subconscious wishes in the familial situation is itself sufficient explanation of taboos. We can see Freud first recognizing that the reality of his postulated historical cause is unimportant and then turning back on himself and deducing the historical event from the psychic system: everyone has these subconscious desires, and not simply as a result of the original deed, which may not have taken place; but primitive men were uninhibited and therefore must have acted. The historical event is asserted as if it were a cause, but then it is inferred from the subconscious system. This is a splendid example of the tension between historical explanation and explanation in terms of a system, and it is especially instructive as a lesson in modernity, because the system wins against Freud's express wishes.

Saussure, Durkheim, and Freud seem responsible for this decisive step in the development of the human sciences. By internalizing origins, removing them from temporal history, one creates a new space of explanation which has come to be called the unconscious. It is not so much that the unconscious replaces the historical series; rather, it becomes the space where any antecedents that have an explanatory function are located. Structural explanation relates actions to a system of norms—the rules of a language, the collective representations of a society, the mechanisms of a psychic economy—and the concept of the unconscious is a way of explaining how these systems have explanatory force. It is a way of explaining how they can be simultaneously unknown yet effectively present. If a description of a linguistic system counts as the analysis of a language, it is because the system is something not immediately given to consciousness yet deemed to be always present, always at work in the behavior it structures and makes possible.

Though the concept of the unconscious as such arises in the work of Freud, it is essential to the type of explanation that a whole range of modern disciplines seek to offer and would certainly have been developed even without Freud's aid. In fact, one could argue that in linguistics the concept emerges in its clearest and most irrefutable form. The unconscious is the concept that enables one to explain an indubitable fact: that I know a language (in the sense that I can produce and understand new utterances, tell whether a sequence is in fact a sentence of my language, etc.), yet I do not know what I know. I know a language; yet I need a linguist to explain to me precisely what it is that I know. The concept of the unconscious connects and makes sense of these two facts and opens a space for exploration. Linguistics, like psychology and a sociology of collective representations, will explain my actions by setting out in detail the implicit knowledge that I myself have not brought to consciousness.

Another way of describing this fundamental step—a way whose importance will become clearer in the next chapter—would be to say that it consists of placing the "subject," or the "I," at the center of one's analytical domain and then dismantling it. "Subject" in this context means the subject of experience, the "I" or self that thinks, perceives, speaks, and so on. Comparative and historical linguistics could be carried out without explicit reference to the subject; one could note the differences between attested forms and follow the evolution of a given form without calling upon or making use of the notion of the subject who speaks, the subject who knows a language. But Saussure puts the subject right at the center of his analytical project. The notion of the subject becomes central to the analysis of language.

How do we identify linguistic units? Always with reference to the speaking subject. We know that /b/ and /p/ are different phonemes because, for the subject, *bet* and *pet* are different signs. The opposition between /b/ and /p/ differentiates signs for the speaker.

What makes two utterances identical? The fact that, despite measurable physical differences, they are identical for the speaking subject. "In order to tell to what extent a thing is a reality," at least from the point of view of synchronic analysis of *la langue,* "it is necessary and sufficient to ask to what extent it exists in the minds of speakers" (*Course,* 90; *Cours,* 128).

In all cases where we are dealing with what Saussure calls values, that is to say with the social significance of objects and actions, the subject takes on a crucial role, in that the facts one is seeking to explain come from the subject's intuitions and judgments. However, once the subject is in place, firmly established at the center of the analytical domain, the whole enterprise of the human sciences becomes one of dismantling the subject, of explaining meanings in terms of systems of convention which escape the subject's conscious grasp. The speaker of a language is not consciously aware of the phonological and grammatical systems, in whose terms judgments and perceptions can be explained. Nor is the subject necessarily aware of its own psychic economy or of the elaborate system of social norms which governs behavior.

The subject is broken down into its constituents, which turn out to be interpersonal systems of convention. It is "dissolved" as its functions are attributed to a variety of systems which operate through it. As Michel Foucault writes, "the researches of psychoanalysis, of linguistics, of anthropology have 'decentered' the subject in relation to the laws of its desire, the forms of its language, the rules of its actions, or the play of its mythical and imaginative discourse." The distinction between the subject and the world is a variable one that depends on the configurations of knowledge at a given time, and the disciplines inaugurated by Saussure, Durkheim, and Freud have chipped away at what previously belonged to the subject, until it has lost its place as center or source of meaning. As it is broken down into component systems that are all transsubjective, the self or subject comes to appear more and more as a construct, the result of systems of conventions. When one speaks, one artfully "complies with language"; language speaks through us as do desire and society. Even the idea of personal identity emerges through the discourse of a culture. The "I" is not something given; it comes to exist, in a mirror stage which starts in infancy, as that which is seen and addressed by others.

The problem of the subject is one to which we shall return when we come to consider some of the implications of semiotics and the ways in which people working in other disciplines have actually been influenced by Saussure and his methodological program. So far, of course, we have not been concerned with problems of influence: there is no evidence that Durkheim, Saussure, or Freud knew anything of each other's work, and though Durkheim's influence on Saussure has been suggested, any resemblances are probably due to their common debt to Taine. In any case, more important than any possible surface borrowings are the affinities between the fundamental projects of these three thinkers, and in particular the epistemological configurations of the disciplines they founded.

I have argued that Saussure is especially interesting and suggestive as an intellectual strategist, as a forceful thinker concerned with fundamentals of method and definition. Yet he is principally known as the founder of modern linguistics, and we must now look at some of the things he instigated in order to see what advances his work helped produce and where his linguistic theories have proven inadequate.

Influence

Saussure's influence on modern linguistics has been of two kinds. First, he provided a general orientation, a sense of the tasks of linguistics which has seldom been questioned, so much has it come to be taken for granted as the very nature of the subject itself. For Saussure, the linguist's task was to analyze a language as a system of units and relations; to do linguistics was to attempt to define the units of a language, the relations between them, and their rules of combination. This sense of the task of linguistics is not found in Saussure's predecessors, though some of them may have made occasional bows in this direction. But since Saussure this has become, very nearly, the definition of linguistic investigation. Not only has descriptive and theoretical linguistics grown in order to take up the central place which Saussure assigns it, but those working in historical linguistics or sociolinguistics are compelled to use adjectives like "historical" to show how their work departs from the central activity of the discipline. Someone who wished to take issue with Saussure's view of the task of linguistics would do so not by attacking Saussure but by challenging the idea of linguistics itself.

It is in this sense that Saussure can be called the founder of modern linguistics. His most important and original contribution is a silent influence which has passed into the nature of the discipline itself. Indeed, an account of structural linguistics as inaugurated by Saussure can include the major schools of modern linguistics. Thus, Giulio Lepschy's *A Survey of Structural Linguistics* covers the Prague School (Roman Jakobson, Nikolai Trubetzkoy, and others), the Copenhagen School (Louis Hjelmslev and other "Glossematicians"), the "Functionalists" (Jakobson, Emile Benveniste, André Martinet, and some contemporary British linguists), American Structuralism (Leonard Bloomfield and his followers), and even Noam Chomsky and other transformational grammarians. Only this last group has altered in a fundamental way the concept of linguistics as bequeathed by Saussure.

There is, however, a second kind of influence worth studying, the influence of specific concepts which are not strictly original to Saussure but which he helped to promote: the distinction between *langue* and *parole,* the separation of the synchronic and the diachronic perspectives, and the view of language as a system of syntagmatic and paradigmatic relations operating at various hierarchical levels. Many of the developments of modern linguistics can be described as investigations of the precise nature and import of these concepts. Considering them in turn, we can see that even when Saussure's original formulations have been found wanting he posed the questions that have animated modern linguistics.

Langue and *Parole*

In 1933 the British linguist Sir Alan Gardiner wrote, "To Ferdinand de Saussure belongs the merit of having drawn attention to the distinction between 'speech' and 'language,' a distinction so far-reaching in its consequences that in my opinion it can hardly fail, sooner or later, to become the indispensable basis of all scientific treatment of grammar." So indispensable has it been that many linguistic disagreements can be cast in the form of disputes about the precise nature of the distinction: what belongs to *langue* and what to *parole?*

Saussure himself invokes various criteria in making the distinction: in separating *langue* from *parole,* one separates the essential from the contingent, the social from the purely individual, and the psychological from the material. But these criteria do not divide language in the same way and they thus leave much room for dispute. By the first, *la langue* is a wholly abstract and formal system; everything relating to sound is relegated to *parole,* since, for example, English would still be essentially the same language even if its units were expressed in some other way. But, clearly, by the second criterion we should have to revise this view: the fact that /b/ is a voiced bilabial stop and a /p/ a voiceless bilabial stop is a fact about the linguistic system, in that individual speakers cannot choose to realize the phonemes differently if they are to continue speaking English. And by the third criterion one would have to admit other acoustic features to *la langue,* since differences between accents and pronunciations have a psychological reality for speakers of a language.

Saussure's distinction has been fruitful through its very openness. In fact, the varied results achieved by applying each criterion reflect different ways in which language can be systematic. We can state these differences in the terms suggested by Hjelmslev: *langue* and *parole* can be replaced by *schema, norm, usage,* and *parole. Parole* is simply the individual speech act and not itself part of the system. Usage is a statistical regularity: one can chart the frequency of different pronunciations or of other uses of linguistic elements. A speaker of a language has a certain freedom in his choice of usage. The norm, however, is not a matter of individual choice. It is not described statistically but represented by a series of rules:

e.g., the phoneme /p/ is realized in English as a voiceless bilabial stop. Finally, with the schema, the most abstract conception of structure, there is no reference to phonic substance.
Elements are defined in abstract relational terms: /p/ is to /b/
as /t/ is to /d/, and it is irrelevant what actual features are used
to manifest these differences.

Given this fourway distinction, one could, in fact, locate
the division between *langue* and *parole* at any of three points:
la langue could consist of schema only, or of schema and
norm, or of schema, norm, and usage. And disputes about the
nature of *la langue* have usually been of this character. Linguists of the Prague School, for example, treated *la langue* as
a combination of schema and norm. Distinguishing between
phonetics and phonology, they argued that phonology should
investigate which phonic differences are linked with differences in meaning, but that the phonological distinctive features thus isolated should be described in articulatory terms.
In Jakobson's influential account of distinctive features, oppositions such as *voiced* versus *voiceless* are not only abstract
features but norms of physical or phonetic realization.

Other linguists, such as Daniel Jones and his British followers, preferred to define the phoneme as a "family" of sounds,
thus including usage within *la langue*: for them, to describe
the phonological system of a language is to describe linguistic
usage as well as functional norms and abstract schemas. On
the other hand, Hjelmslev and the exponents of his Glosse-
matics treated *la langue* purely as an abstract schema. For
them, phonetic properties are not at all involved in the way in
which phonemes should be described. These disputes continue, but at least in the realm of phonology, the essential
questions were posed by Saussure's distinction between
langue and *parole*.

At the syntactic level Saussure's views on what belongs to
la langue and what to *parole* are more obscure, indecisive,
and questionable. He thinks of sentences as the products of

individual choice and therefore treats them as instances of *parole* rather than entities of *la langue*. One is tempted to say that he failed to distinguish between sentences themselves as grammatical forms and the utterances by which sentences are realized in speech; but the problem goes deeper than this. Set idiomatic phrases, he allows, are part of the linguistic system, and even "sentences and groups of words built on regular patterns," but he seems unwilling to consider how far the notion of "regular pattern" can be extended, and he concludes that on the plane of syntagmatic combinations "there is no clear-cut boundary between facts of *la langue*, which are examples of collective usage, and facts of *parole*, which depend on the free choice of the individual" (*Course*, 125; *Cours*, 173).

Because of his failure to include sentences within the linguistic system, Saussure's conception of syntax seems exceptionally weak. Language is more than a system of interrelated units; the relations which compose it are also a system of rules, and it is this aspect that Chomsky stresses in replacing Saussure's *langue* and *parole* with his own concepts of *competence* and *performance*. Competence is the underlying system of rules that a speaker has mastered, and to describe competence is to analyze a language into its elements and their rules of combination. "Clearly," Chomsky writes, "the description of intrinsic competence provided by the grammar is not to be confused with an account of actual performance, as de Saussure emphasized with such lucidity." But Saussure, he continues,

> regards *langue* as basically a store of signs with their grammatical properties, that is, a store of word-like elements, fixed phrases, and, perhaps, certain limited phrase types. He was thus quite unable to come to grips with the recursive processes underlying sentence formation, and he appears to regard sentence formation as a

matter of *parole* rather than *langue*, of free and voluntary creation rather than systematic rule. There is no place in his scheme for "rule-governed creativity" of the kind involved in the ordinary everyday use of language.[6]

It is worth noting, however, that it is precisely because Saussure recognized the creativity of ordinary language use that he was unwilling to include sentence formation in *la langue*. He did not know how to reconcile the fact that we can produce totally new sentences with the fact that a language contains phrase types. What he lacked was a notion of rule-governed creativity: individual creativity made possible by a system of rules. He did not realize that it is possible to construct a finite set of rules that will generate structural descriptions for an infinite number of sentences. This can be done, as Chomsky says, by recursive rules: rules that can be applied over and over again, such as the rule which enables one to attach a relative clause to a noun phrase (e.g., This is the dog that chased the cat that worried the rat that ate the cheese, and so on).

People who know a language can recognize whether a sentence they have never before encountered is formed in accordance with the rules of that language and can themselves produce new sentences which accord with the grammar. This is sufficient proof that the sentence must be considered a unit of the linguistic system. It was left to Chomsky to show how the system could account for sentence formation while at the same time accounting for the creativity of individual speakers. Saussure's inability to do this is quite understandable, and he does seem at least to have understood the nature of the problem, but his neglect of the sentence as a linguistic unit is nevertheless an important failure; in the area of syntax,

[6]*Current Issues in Linguistic Theory* (The Hague: Mouton, 1964), p. 23. For further discussion of Chomsky's theories and his place in the history of linguistics, see John Lyons, *Chomsky* (New York: Viking, 1970).

more than anywhere else, Saussure's approach to language has been superseded.[7]

Synchronic and Diachronic

Of all Saussure's distinctions this has been least clearly understood and least perceptively investigated by his successors. Though the priority of synchronic description has been accepted, little attempt has been made to clarify the basic theoretical problem Saussure posed—about what precisely belongs to the synchronic and what to the diachronic perspective in discussions of linguistic change. Many linguists have asserted that one must overcome or transcend the distinction and achieve a global, synthetic view of language, but they have not come to terms with the reasons Saussure offers for thinking this impossible; and Charles Hockett was doubtless correct to observe in his survey of linguistics, *The State of the Art* (1968), that the problem of the relationship between synchronic and diachronic studies "had been not so much settled as swept under the rug."

Two sorts of claim are made by those who seek to overcome the distinction between the synchronic and the diachronic. The first is that at any moment the synchronic system contains diachronic elements: archaisms, neologisms, distinctions in the process of disappearing, and so on. This objection is irrelevant to Saussure's point. He explicitly states that "at every moment a language implies an established system and an evolution; at every moment it is a present institution and a product of the past." Synchronic and diachronic are not two types of element but two approaches to language. Items experienced as archaic at a given moment will be so identified in a synchronic analysis, but this has nothing to do

[7]However, Wallis Reid argues that Saussure's weakness is really a strength: "The Saussurian Sign as a Control in Linguistic Analysis," *Semiotexte* 1, no. 2 (1974).

with historical investigation (it would make no difference to the synchronic description, for example, if forms that speakers felt to be archaic were really new borrowings from another language).

The other kind of objection is more apposite and interesting. Linguists of the Prague School insisted that linguistic change was not a blind force but fundamentally systematic: that it was a function of the system. And recently those working on phonology in the context of transformational grammar have taken an anti-Saussurian position. Whereas Saussure maintains that sound change takes place outside the linguistic system, with external factors affecting *parole*, other linguists now argue that sound change arises within the linguistic system itself, can operate on grammatically defined elements, and is best described as a change in rules, not as the evolution of realization elements. For example, at one point the *k* in forms like *knowledge* was pronounced. The sound change which affected *kn* seems to have depended on grammatical structure, so that the *k* is sounded in *acknowledge* but not in *a knowledge*.

The evidence is not conclusive, for there are other, albeit *ad hoc* ways of explaining such changes. Nor is it clear whether Saussure's opposition to teleological notions of change—that change occurs because the system "seeks" a different state—needs to be abandoned. Certainly, many changes are not explicable in teleological terms: one cannot argue that the "inadequacy" of *fōt/fōti* led the system to seek *foot/feet* as a way of marking plurals. And it may be that the evidence cited as counter-examples often results from a failure to distinguish the synchronic facts of language change from the diachronic. In general, the relation between the synchronic and the diachronic is a problem that has not been sufficiently explored, and here Saussure's position, as it was expounded (pp. 45–56), is as clear and apposite a formulation of the central difficulties as has yet been produced.

Ferdinand de Saussure

Relations in the Linguistic System

Saussure asserted unequivocally that language is a system of differences in which all elements are defined solely by their relations with one another. He reached this conclusion, it will be recalled, by reflecting on the nature of identity in linguistics and on the properties of the linguistic sign. From a theoretical point of view his conclusion seems irreproachable, and it has exercised considerable influence. But when one actually analyzes a language it becomes extremely difficult to avoid speaking as if there were positive terms. It is difficult to analyze a language purely as a system of relations. How far this difficulty has significant theoretical implications is not clear, but it is true to say that linguists have been more successful in investigating particular types of relations or restricted sets of relations than in treating an entire language as a purely relational system.

For example, the prominence Saussure gives to binary oppositions has borne fruit. Most work in phonology has been based on a reduction of the sound continuum to discrete elements which can be defined as the point of intersection of several distinctive features. Each distinctive feature, as Jakobson says, involves the choice between "two terms of an opposition that displays a specific differential property" (e.g., *voiced* as opposed to *voiceless*). Indeed, Jakobson and others argue that the use of binary oppositions to describe structure is not simply a methodological device but a reflection of the nature of language itself. Binary oppositions are the most natural and economical code; they are the first operations children learn as they begin to accede to language; and, more generally, they are the common denominator of all thought. Once again we see Saussure and the Saussurian tradition reestablishing links between language and thought, but at the level of fundamental structuring operations.

Syntagmatic and paradigmatic relations have also been the focus of attention for many linguists, and one could argue that the differences between the various theories of grammatical description that have grown up since Saussure's day are essentially disagreements about the nature of syntagmatic relations and ways of determining them. These disagreements are not of a sort that could be succinctly summarized here. Suffice it to say the concept of a hierarchy of linguistic levels, in which constituents of one level (such as phonemes) combine to form constituents of the next level (such as morphemes) and in which the combinatory potential of elements serves to define them, is common to a range of descriptive theories, which differ in their judgments about the weight to be given to various factors in determining relations. Should one, for example, take similar utterances and, treating them as sequences of forms, divide them at points where they differ from one another, and then study the combinations which the elements so isolated enter in other sequences? Or should one begin with a theory of the various functions which linguistic elements can perform and then identify the elements that combine to perform them?

Only with the advent of Chomsky's transformational-generative grammar has the importance of syntagmatic and paradigmatic elements, as defined by Saussure, been reduced. And even there the problem has been only displaced: various kinds of paradigmatic classes do emerge, as the classes on which rules operate, as the classes which are necessary if the rules are to operate properly. And the rules themselves are representations of what Saussure would have seen as syntagmatic relations, had he extended his account of relations to make adequate provision for syntactic processes.

Moreover, the recent work of transformational grammarians returns, though at a different level, to the view expressed by Saussure that when one thinks rigorously about combinatory processes, taking nothing for granted, one discovers no essential difference between morphological combinations and other syntactic combinations. For Saussure, this is an inference only; his remarks on syntax are so sketchy that they offer no support for his claim. But now, just as the discovery of Hittite confirmed Saussure's hypothesis about Indo-European vowels, so transformational grammar may demonstrate the correctness of another postulate or insight.

In one respect, however, the father of modern linguistics would have been disappointed in his children. Saussure maintained that linguistics was a branch of semiology, the general science of signs and systems of signs. Linguistics belongs not to the natural sciences, nor to the historical sciences, but to semiology. "For me the problem of language is above all semiological. . . . If we wish to discover the true nature of the linguistic system, we must first study what it has in common with other systems of the same type" (*Course*, 17; *Cours*, 34–35). This advice, this program, has been ignored by linguists. While other Saussurian concepts have been assimilated, Saussure's ruling concept, the notion of the sign and of language as a system of signs, has been largely neglected. Linguists have paid lip service to the concept but have not allowed it to govern their analysis of a language. It can be argued that if the sign were granted the role it has in Saussure this would lead to an important reorientation of linguistics, but until the attempt is made one cannot say what its consequences would be.[8] What one can say is that linguists' failure to make the sign an object of attention has led to an anomalous situation: semiotics, as it is now generally called, has been embraced by people working in many different fields, but linguistics itself, which Saussure placed at the center of semiotics and to which he thought semiotics would make a major contribution, remains aloof. Linguistics has developed in a Saussurian way, but to understand the context within which Saussure placed it we must abandon the study of language as such, and look at attempts to study other social and cultural phenomena as "languages," as systems of signs.

[8] For discussion of this question, see Reid, "The Saussurian Sign."

4

Semiotics: The Saussurian Legacy

Very few paragraphs of the *Course in General Linguistics* are devoted to semiotics, and this is no doubt one reason why linguists generally neglected to follow Saussure's lead in developing a general science of signs that would situate and orient linguistics. But for Saussure the semiotic perspective was central to any serious study of language. "Is it not obvious," he wrote, "that language is above all a system of signs and that therefore we must have recourse to the science of signs" if we are to define it properly? (Engler, 47).

Language is a system of signs that express ideas and is thus comparable to the system of writing, to the alphabet of deaf-mutes, to symbolic rituals, to forms of etiquette, to military signals, etc. It is but the most important of these systems.

We can therefore imagine a *science which would study the life of signs within society.* . . . We call it *semiology*, from the Greek *semeion* ("sign"). It would teach us what signs consist of, what laws govern them. Since it does not yet exist, we cannot say what it will be; but it has a right to existence; its place is assured in advance. Linguistics is only a part of this general science; and the laws which semiology discovers will be applicable to linguistics, which will thus find itself attached to a well-defined domain of human phenomena. (*Course,* 16; *Cours,* 33)

Since human beings make noises, use gestures, employ combinations of objects or actions in order to convey meaning, there is a place for a discipline which would analyze this kind of activity and make explicit the systems of convention on which it rests. And, Saussure argues, if linguistics is conceived as a part of semiology, there will be important consequences:

> aspects of language which may at first seem extremely important (such as the use of vocal mechanisms) will become secondary considerations if they serve only to distinguish language from other semiological systems. This procedure will not only clarify the problems of linguistics; rituals, customs, etc., will, we believe, appear in a new light if they are studied as signs, and one will come to see that they should be included in the domain of semiology and explained by its laws. (*Course,* 17; *Cours,* 35)

Semiotics is thus based on the assumption that insofar as human actions or productions convey meaning, insofar as they function as signs, there must be an underlying system of conventions and distinctions which makes this meaning possible. Where there are signs there is system. This is what various signifying activities have in common, and if one is to determine their essential nature, one must treat them not in isolation but as examples of semiotic systems. In this way, aspects that are often hidden or neglected will become apparent, especially when nonlinguistic signifying practices are considered as "languages."

But why should linguistics, the study of one particular

though very important signifying system, be thought to provide the model for studying other systems? Why should linguistics be, as Saussure called it, "le patron général" of semiology? The answer takes us back to a familiar starting point, the arbitrary nature of the sign.

Linguistics may serve as a model for semiology, Saussure argued, because in the case of language the arbitrary and conventional nature of the sign is especially clear. Nonlinguistic signs may often seem natural to those who use them, and it may require some effort to see that the politeness or impoliteness of an action is not a necessary and intrinsic property of that action but a conventional meaning. But if linguistics is taken as a model it will compel analysts to attend to the conventional basis of the nonlinguistic signs they are studying.

This is not to say that all signs are wholly arbitrary. There are some intrinsic constraints on the meanings actions can bear and, reciprocally, on the class of actions appropriate to express a particular meaning. It is difficult to imagine a culture where a punch in the mouth might be a friendly greeting, but, within limits, a whole range of actions would serve perfectly well as friendly greetings. Within this realm of available possibilities one can speak of signs as conventional and arbitrary. Saussure writes:

> Every means of expression used in a society is based, in principle, on a collective norm—in other words, on convention. Signs of politeness, for instance, often have a certain natural expressivity (one thinks of the way a Chinese prostrates himself nine times before the emperor by way of salutation), but they are nonetheless determined by a rule; and it is this rule which leads one to use them, not their intrinsic value. We can therefore say that wholly arbitrary signs are those which come closest to the semiological ideal. This is why language, the most complex and widespread of systems of expression, is

also the most characteristic. And for this reason linguistics can serve as a model for semiology as a whole, though language is only one of its systems. (*Course*, 68; *Cours*, 100–101)

The virtue of taking linguistics as a model for semiotic analysis lies in the presumption it establishes: that signs will be arbitrary and conventional.

Why is this important? Signs frequently seem natural—endowed with inherent meaning—to those who use them. People are inclined to insist that their own behavior is governed by practical rather than symbolic considerations, contending that they choose clothes that are "comfortable" or "of good quality," buy food whose taste they like, and use gestures that are naturally expressive. The more powerful a culture, the more it succeeds in having its signs taken as natural. Semiotic analysis, therefore, requires a model that insists on the conventional, cultural basis of signs so as to resist the ideological forces that naturalize them. If one starts with the presumption that signs are arbitrary, one will be disposed to seek out the underlying systems of convention. Just as, in linguistics, the arbitrary nature of the sign leads one to elucidate the system of functional differences that create signs, so in other cases one will focus on significant differences: differences and oppositions which bear meaning. What differentiates a polite from an impolite greeting, a fashionable from an unfashionable garment? One comes to study not isolated signs but a system of distinctions.

The Domain of Semiotics

Saussure's proposals concerning semiology were not immediately taken up, and only toward the middle of this century, many years after the publication of the *Course*, did others begin to realize the importance of his suggestions. It is as if the individual disciplines had to develop in their own ways and rediscover Saussure's insights for themselves before they could become properly semiotic. Indeed, what is now called "structuralism" arose when anthropologists, literary critics, and others saw that the example of linguistics could help to justify what they sought to do in their own disciplines; and as they began to take linguistics as a model, they realized that they were in fact developing the semiology which Saussure had so long ago proposed.

Thus, it was not until 1961, in his inaugural lecture at the Collège de France, that the anthropologist Claude Lévi-Strauss defined anthropology as a branch of semiology and paid homage to Saussure as the pioneer who had laid the foundations for the proper conception of anthropology. But fifteen years earlier, in an epoch-making article, "Structural Analysis in Linguistics and Anthropology," Lévi-Strauss had already drawn upon the concepts and methods of linguistics to establish his brand of structuralism.

In this article, Lévi-Strauss speaks of the advances in linguistics, especially in phonology, which have made it a scientific discipline and remarks that "phonology cannot help but play the same renovating role for the social sciences that nuclear physics, for example, played for the exact sciences." He proposes that anthropology follow the example of linguistics and reproduce in its own field something comparable to the "phonological revolution." Phonology studies relations between terms, systems of relations, and passes from the study of phenomena that are consciously grasped or known by speakers of a language to their "unconscious infrastructure." That is to say, it seeks to identify systems of relations that are known only subconsciously. What lesson can anthropology draw from this? It is, Lévi-Strauss says, an example in method: in order to analyze signifying phenomena, in order to investigate actions or objects which bear meaning, one should postulate the existence of an underlying system of relations and try to see whether the meaning of individual elements or objects is not a result of their contrasts with other elements and objects in a system of relations of which members of a culture are not consciously aware.[1]

Nikolai Trubetzkoy, in his seminal work, *Principles of Phonology* (1939), had already outlined the methodological implications of phonological theory for the social sciences and thus had advanced the semiology proposed by Saussure. While the phonetician is concerned with the properties of actual speech sounds, the phonologist is interested in the differential features that are functional in a particular language, asking what phonic differences are linked with differences of meaning, how the differential elements are related to one another, and how they combine to form words or phrases. It is clear, Trubetzkoy continues, that these tasks cannot be accomplished by the methods of the natural sciences, which are concerned with the intrinsic properties of natural phenomena themselves and not with the differential features that bear social significance. In other words, in the natural sciences there is nothing corresponding to the distinction between *langue* and *parole*: there is no institution or conventional system to be studied. The social and human sciences, on the other hand, are concerned with the social use of material objects and must therefore distinguish between the objects themselves and the system of distinctive or differential features that gives them meaning and value.

Attempts to describe such systems, Trubetzkoy argues, are closely analogous to work in phonology. The example he cites is the study of clothing, as it might be carried out by an anthropologist or a sociologist. Many features of physical garments themselves which would be of great importance to the wearer are of no interest to the anthropologist, who is

[1]Lévi-Strauss's essay can be found in *Structural Anthropology* (New York: Basic Books, 1963).

concerned only with those features that carry a social significance. Thus, the length of skirts might carry a lot of significance in the social system of a culture, while the material from which they were made did not. Or again, if I were to wear a yellow suit rather than a gray suit it might have considerable social meaning, but the facts that I have a strong preference for gray suits rather than brown suits or a dislike for woolen materials might be purely personal preferences with no social significance. Just as phonologists try to determine which differences in sound bear meaning and which do not, so anthropologists or sociologists studying clothes would try to isolate those features of garments which carried social significance. They attempt to reconstruct the system of relations and distinctions which members of a society have assimilated and which they display in taking certain garments as indicating a particular life-style, social role, or social attitude. In short, they are interested in those features by which garments are made into signs.

Like linguists, the anthropologists or sociologists are attempting to make explicit the implicit knowledge that enables people within a given society to communicate and understand each other's behavior. The facts they are trying to explain are facts about implicit knowledge: that a particular action is regarded as polite while another is impolite; that a particular garment is appropriate in one situation but inappropriate in another. Where there is knowledge or mastery of any kind, there is a system to be explained. This is the fundamental principle that guides the extrapolation from linguistics into other disciplines. If the meanings that members of a culture assign to objects or actions are not purely random, then there must be a semiotic system of distinctions, categories, and rules of combination, which one might hope to describe.

One could thus assign to semiotics a vast field of inquiry: if everything that has meaning within a culture is a sign and therefore an object of semiotic investigation, semiotics would come to include most disciplines of the humanities and the social sciences. Any domain of human activity—be it music, architecture, cooking, etiquette, advertising, fashion, literature—could be approached in semiotic terms.

The immediate objection to an imperialistic semiotics, which sought in this way to encompass so many other disciplines, might be that the signifying phenomena one encounters in these various domains are not all alike. Even if most objects and activities are signs, they are not signs of the same type. This is an important objection, and one of the major tasks of semiotics is to distinguish between different types of sign, which may need to be studied in different ways.

Various typologies of signs have been proposed, but three fundamental classes of signs stand out as requiring different approaches: the icon, the index, and the sign proper (sometimes misleadingly called "symbol"). All signs consist of a signifier and a signified, a form and an associated meaning or meanings; but the relations between signifier and signified are different for each of these three types of sign. An *icon* involves actual resemblance between signifier and signified: a portrait signifies the person of whom it is a portrait less by an arbitrary convention than by resemblance. In an *index* the relation between signifier and signified is causal: smoke means fire because fire is generally the cause of smoke; clouds mean rain if they are the sort of clouds that produce rain; tracks are signs of the type of animal likely to have produced them. In the *sign proper*, however, the relation between signifier and signified is arbitrary and conventional: shaking hands conventionally signifies greeting; cheese is by convention an appropriate food with which to end a meal.

What are the implications of this three-way division for semiotics? The main consequence is to make the sign proper the central object of semiotics and to make the study of other signs a specialized and secondary activity. Studying how a drawing or photograph of a horse represents a horse might form part of semiotics, but it seems more properly the concern of a philosophical theory of representation than of a linguistically based semiotics. Semiotics must identify and characterize iconic signs, but the study of icons is not likely to be one of its central activities.

Indices are more worrying. If one places them within the domain of semiotics, then it seems to take all human knowledge for its province; for any science which attempts to establish causal relations among phenomena could be seen as a study of indices and thus placed within semiotics. Medicine, for example, tries to relate diseases to symptoms: to have discovered the symptoms of a disease is to have identified the signs which betray the presence of that disease and, reciprocally, to have learned what these symptoms are signs of. Meteorology attempts to construct a system in order to relate atmospheric conditions to their causes and consequences and thus to read them as signs: as signs of weather conditions. Economic prediction depends on a proper reading of economic signs: economics is the discipline which identifies these signs and enables one to read them. In short, a whole range of disciplines try to decipher the natural or social world; the methods of these disciplines are different, and there is no reason to think that they would gain substantially by being brought under the banner of an imperialistic semiotics.

Signs proper, where the relation between signifier and signified is arbitrary or conventional, are, then, the central domain of semiotics. They require semiotic investigation if their mechanisms are to be understood. In the absence of a causal link between signifier and signified, which would enable one to treat each sign individually, one must try to reconstruct the semiotic system, the system of conventions, from which a whole group of signs derive. Precisely because the individual signs are unmotivated, one must attempt to reconstruct the system, which alone can explain them.

However, one cannot exclude indices altogether from the domain of semiotics, for they form an interesting and important borderline case. The fact is that any index may be used as a conventional sign. Once the causal or indexical relationship between a signifier and a signified is recognized by a culture, the particular signifier becomes associated with its signified and can be used to evoke that meaning even in cases where the causal relation is absent. Once it is generally recognized that smoke means fire, I can use smoke produced by a smoke machine to signify fire, even though the smoke is not in this case being caused by fire. The index is here being used as a conventional sign.

Many indices, of course, can be used as conventional signs in this theatrical way: if an actor is made up to look as if he had measles, we read his spots as signifying measles in a conventional way and do not believe that the spots are in his case causally connected with measles. But there is a large set of conventionalized indices which are especially interesting to the semiotician because they come to constitute the conventional social mythology of a culture. What we call "status symbols" are perhaps the best example. These are not just indices of status but symbols of status; though they have some causal or intrinsic relation to the status they signify, they have been promoted by the conventions of a society to the rank of symbol and carry more meaning than their causal or indexical nature would entail. Thus, a Rolls-Royce is certainly an index of wealth in that one must be wealthy to own one, but social convention has made it a symbol of wealth, a mythical object that signifies wealth more imperiously than other objects which might be equally expensive. Among the many objects which are indices of wealth in that they are all expensive, it has been singled out by social usage as a symbol of wealth. A semiotics studying social life as a system of signs will certainly want to include conventionalized indices of this kind within its domain.[2]

Indices also enter the domain of semiotics in another way. Within particular sciences the meanings of indices change with the configurations of knowledge. Medical symptoms, for example, are read and interpreted differently from one era to another as knowledge advances. There are changes both in what are identified as symptoms and in the way symptoms are interpreted. It thus becomes possible for semiotics to study the changes in medicine as an interpretive system, as a way of reading and identifying signs. It would be trying to discover the conventions that determine or make possible the medical discourse of a period and permit indices to be read. In this investigation the semiotician would be interested not in the symptoms or indices themselves, nor in the "real" causal relation between index and meaning, but in the reading of indices within a system of conventions.

What then is the domain of semiotics? How far does its empire extend? It will obviously have variable boundaries; there are many things that can be treated semiotically but that need not necessarily be studied in this way. In fact, to characterize the domain of semiotics, one must simply identify the different sorts of cases it can encounter.

(1) At the heart of the semiotic enterprise are systems of conventional signs used for direct communication. These include, first, the various codes used to convey messages composed in an existing natural language, such as English. Morse code, semaphore codes, braille, and all the codes devised for secrecy can be used to convey an English message. Second, there is a whole series of specialized codes used to convey a particular type of information to groups who may not share the same natural language: chemical symbols, traffic signals

[2]For this aspect of semiotics see Roland Barthes, *Mythologies* (New York: Hill & Wang, 1972), especially the important theoretical discussion in the final essay.

and road signs, silver assay marks, mathematical symbols, the signs used in airports, trains, etc., and finally the recondite symbolisms of heraldic or alchemical codes.[3] All these cases involve conventional signs based on explicit codes: since they are designed for easy and unambiguous communication, there is an explicit procedure for encoding and decoding, such as looking up the item in question in a code book. Such codes are pure examples of semiotic systems, but precisely because they are so straightforward it is usually an easy matter to describe the principles on which they are constructed, and so they often prove much less interesting than less explicit and more complicated systems which fall into our next category.

(2) More complicated than explicit codes are systems where communication undoubtedly takes place, but where the codes on which the communication depends are difficult to establish and highly ambiguous or openended. Such is the case, for example, with literature. To read and understand literature, one requires more than a knowledge of the language in which it is written; but it is very difficult to establish precisely *what* supplementary knowledge is required. Certainly, one is not dealing with the sort of codes for which keys or code books could be supplied. However, precisely because one is dealing with an extremely rich and complicated communicative system, the semiotic study of literature and other aesthetic codes (such as those of painting and music) can be extraordinarily interesting.

The reason for the evasive complexity of these codes is quite simple. Codes of the first type are designed to communicate directly and unambiguously messages and notions which are already known; the code simply provides an economical notation for notions that are already defined. But aesthetic expression aims to communicate notions, subtleties,

---

[3]Many systems of this sort are discussed by Georges Mounin, *Introduction à la sémiologie* (Paris: Minuit, 1970).

complexities that have not yet been formulated, and, therefore, as soon as an aesthetic code comes to be generally perceived as a code (as a way of expressing notions which have already been articulated), then works of art tend to move beyond it. They question, parody, and generally undermine it, while exploring its possible mutations and extensions. One might even say that much of the interest of works of art lies in the ways in which they explore and modify the codes they seem to be using; this makes semiotic investigation of these systems both highly relevant and extremely difficult.

(3) The third case that semiotics must confront covers social practices which may not at first seem to involve communication but which are highly codified, and which certainly employ a whole series of distinctions in order to create meaning. Ritual and etiquette of various kinds and the systems of convention governing food and clothing are obviously semiotic systems: to wear one set of clothes rather than another is to communicate something, albeit indirectly. But one can go further and say that the buildings we inhabit, the objects we purchase, and the actions we perform are of interest to the semiotician, because all the categories and operations through which they are invested with meaning are fundamentally semiotic. This is not to say that purchasing a house, for example, is primarily or essentially a communicative action, but only that the difference between houses is invested with meaning by a semiotic system, and that in choosing one house rather than another, one is dealing with the image projected by the particular house (a country cottage, a brownstone, a crumbling two-family Victorian). One may, for purely practical reasons, choose to purchase a house whose image seems uncongenial, but one is nonetheless involved in a semiotic system. The task of the analyst in dealing with clothing, commercial objects, pastimes, and other cultural artifacts and activities is to make explicit the implicit meanings they seem to bear and to reconstruct the system of connotations on which these meanings are based.

(4) Finally, there are the cases I initially set aside as involving indices rather than signs proper: the disciplines of the social and natural sciences which try to establish relations of cause and effect between phenomena and for which the meaning of an object or an action is likely to be its causal antecedent or consequence, its significance in a causal scheme. As I have mentioned, though these disciplines are not in themselves semiotic, that does not mean that they need escape the attention of the semiotician. The objects these disciplines study are not signs proper; but, the disciplines themselves, as "languages" or systems of articulation, may be studied as semiotic systems.

This is obvious in the case of sciences that are now discredited, such as astrology. Since we do not believe in the causal relations which astrologists established between the movements of the planets and the events of people's lives, it is easy to consider astrology as a system of conventions. The semiotician studying astrology would ask what were the rules or conventions that astrologers employed in attributing meaning to the configurations of the heavens. What were the conventions that one had to accept to be an astrologer?

We would not hesitate to admit that we are dealing here with a system of signs which might be elucidated. But in fact, if we think about the matter, we can see that our semiotic analysis would not be fundamentally affected if future discoveries were to prove that everything the astrologers had said were true. The same rules would still underlie astrological discourse, whether the predictions they yield are true or false. And so we can extend the bounds of semiotics somewhat further: semiotics can study the conventions that govern the discourse and interpretations of any discipline. But notice what this involves. To the semiotician the truth or falsity of the propositions of a discipline will be irrelevant. If everything which botany now asserts were to be disproved, this would not affect a semiotic analysis of the conventions of botany as a system of signs. Botany is not the sum of true statements about plants but a system of discourse. At any given period, a great many things could be truly said about plants which do not fall within the realm of botany (e.g., that roses are systematically cultivated and dandelions systematically uprooted), and the semiotician is interested in the conventions which exclude some statements from the realm of botany and permit others. Though some disciplines—such as medicine, meteorology, psychoanalysis, and astrology—might lend themselves more easily to a semiotic analysis, in that they are more obviously concerned with the reading and interpretation of signs, in fact at this level any system of discourse can be studied semiotically since it is itself a system of signs.

Semiotic Analysis

Linguistics has served as the model for semiotics and, as Saussure suggested, has drawn attention to the conventional nature of signs and the differential nature of meaning. But it will perhaps be evident from the diversity of the sign systems I have mentioned that the concepts and techniques of linguistic analysis may be much better suited for the investigation of some systems than of others. In all cases the analyst distinguishes *langue* from *parole*, tries to go behind the actions or objects themselves to the system of rules and relations which enables them to have meaning. In most cases one will be able to identify syntagmatic and paradigmatic relations: the relations between elements which can be combined to form higher-level units and relations between elements which can replace one another and which therefore contrast with one another to produce meaning. But in some systems the syntax is so weak as to make syntagmatic relations almost nonexistent. Traffic signs, for example, generally do not involve the combination of more than one unit or, if they do (as in signs where the shape indicates the presence of a hazard and the device specifies the sort of hazard), the syntagmatic relation is very simple and uninteresting. Alternatively, in some systems the set of elementary paradigmatic oppositions is extremely limited. In Morse code, for example, there are only two oppositions: noise versus pause and short versus long. Other systems are semantically very weak. The abominations of Leviticus list the animals one is permitted and forbidden to eat. One can, with some ingenuity, reconstruct the system of rules that assign significance to particular animals, but this system produces only two meanings: clean and unclean (i.e., permitted and forbidden).

But for most systems there do seem to be syntagmatic relations, paradigmatic contrasts, and a variety of meanings that can be produced by contrasts and relations. In the food system, for example, one defines on the syntagmatic axis the combinations of courses which can make up meals of different sorts; and each course or slot can be filled by one of many dishes which are in paradigmatic contrast with one another (one wouldn't combine roast beef and lamb chops in a single meal: they would be alternatives on any menu). Those dishes which are alternatives to one another often bear different meanings in that they connote varying degrees of luxury, elegance, and so forth.

Many semiotic systems are complicated by the fact that they rest on other systems, particularly that of language, and thus become "second-order" systems. Literature is one such system: it has language as its basis, and its supplementary conventions are conventions about special uses of language. Thus, to take a simple example, rhetorical figures such as metaphor, metonymy, hyperbole, synecdoche can be seen as operations of a second-order literary code. When Shakespeare writes "But thy eternal summer shall not fade," his words are signs that have a literal meaning in the linguistic

code of English; but the rhetorical figure of metaphor is part
of a second-order literary code which allows one to use the
linguistic signs, *eternal summer*, to mean something like "a
full, languorous beauty that will always remain at its peak."
And furthermore, a convention of love poetry makes hyper-
bolic compliment of this kind, drawing upon metaphors of
nature and natural processes, an appropriate form of praise.

Now it is obvious that the system of literature—the
knowledge one must acquire, over and above knowledge of
the language, in order to read and interpret literary works—
does not involve explicit codes like those of traffic signs and
etiquette. One can learn about various ways of interpreting
figurative language, about the conventions governing different literary genres, about types of literary structure or organization. But literature continually undermines, parodies, and
escapes anything that threatens to become a rigid code or explicit rules for interpretation. Traffic signs do not violate the
code of traffic signs, but literary works are continually
violating codes. This is because literature is fundamentally an
exploration of the possibilities of experience, a questioning of
the categories in and through which we ordinarily view ourselves and the world. Literary codes have an important role in
that they make possible this process of questioning or exploration, just as rules of etiquette make it possible to be impolite. But literary works never lie wholly within the codes that
define them, and this is what makes the semiotic investigation
of literature such a tantalizing enterprise.[4]

In a series of unpublished reflections on medieval German
legends, Saussure shows his interest in the semiotics of literature and his awareness of some of the problems it poses. A
legend, he writes, "is composed of a series of symbols in a
sense which remains to be defined." These symbols, though

[4]For the structuralist and semiotic study of literature, see my *Structuralist Poetics: Structuralism, Linguistics, and the Study of Literature* (Ithaca:
Cornell University Press, 1975).

more difficult to define than the units of a language, are doubtless governed by the same principles as other signs, and "they all form part of semiology."[5] In the case of literature, as in that of language and other semiotic systems, the fundamental problem is one of identity. One is not dealing with fixed signs, such that a given form will always have the same meaning wherever it appears. On the contrary, the literary work is always drawing upon signs which exist prior to it, "combining them and continually drawing from them new meaning." Indeed, considering the problem of characters in his German legends, Saussure reaches the conclusion that one is confronted with a whole series of elements (proper names, attributes, relations with other characters, actions), and that what one speaks of as the character himself or herself is the creation of the reader, the result of drawing together and combining all the disparate elements that readers encounter as they proceed through the text.[6]

Saussure has here hit upon an important system of convention in literature. The production of characters is governed by cultural models that enable us, for example, to infer motives from action or the qualities of a person from manner and appearance. And so if we say that in the course of a given novel or story a character changes, what we are saying is that, in terms of our literary models of character, two actions or attributes which are attached to a single character are in opposition, are incompatible: according to our notions of character, if someone first does X and later does Y we can only make sense of this by saying that the character has changed.

[5]Jean Starobinski, *Words upon Words* (New Haven: Yale University Press, 1979), p. 5. Starobinski prints materials from Saussure's notebooks on legends as well as his discussions of anagrams.

[6]Quoted in D'Arco Silvio Avalle, "La Sémiologie de la narrativité chez Saussure," in *Essais de la théorie du texte,* ed. C. Bouazis (Paris: Galilée, 1973), p. 33.

Anagrams and Logocentrism

Saussure's remarks on the semiology of literature are sketchy though perceptive, but to another, closely related enterprise he devoted much time in his later years and left voluminous notes, although he never ventured to publish anything on the subject. He developed the theory that Latin poets deliberately concealed anagrams of proper names in their verses. He believed he had discovered a supplementary sign system, a special set of conventions for the production of meaning, and he filled many notebooks with remarks on the various types of repetition and anagrams he had discovered (letters dispersed through the text, sometimes in their correct order, sometimes with a change of order, sometimes in pairs or triplets, etc.). Thus the line "Taurasia Cisauna Samnio cepit" is, he writes, "an anagrammatic line containing the entire name of *Scipio* (in the syllables *ci + pi + io*, in addition to the *S* of *Samnio cepit*, which is the first letter of a group in which almost the entire word *Scipio* appears . . .)."[7] Or again, in the thirteen opening lines of Lucretius's *De Rerum Natura*, which are an invocation to Venus, Saussure discovered three anagrams of this goddess's Greek name, Aphrodite.

This example is quite typical: Saussure looked for anagrams of proper names that were relevant to the verses, and he was interested in anagrams that were repeated in a text, not just in occasional anagrams. He amassed an impressive collection of examples and hypotheses about rules governing sound patterning, but there were two considerations that worried him and made him leave his speculations unpublished. First, the question of intention was crucial: if this really were a convention of Latin poetry—a convention poets followed—then why were there no references to the

[7] Starobinski, p. 16.

practice or discussions of it in classical texts? Second, the advice he sought about the statistical probability of the anagrams he discovered was inconclusive. He confronted a paradoxical situation, as he wryly observed: if one finds few anagrams, then these can be dismissed as the results of chance; if one finds many, then that suggests that they are all too easy to find, a commonplace product of the repetition of twenty-six letters.[8] As he wrote in a letter, "I make no secret of the fact that I myself am perplexed—about the most important point: that is, how should one judge the reality or phantasmagoria of the whole question."[9]

The important question, of course, is what are we to think of it? Was it "la folie de Saussure," as it has been called, a crazy obsession, or was it, as others have argued, a radical critique of language and in particular of the sign? Was Saussure obsessed by a chimerical problem, or was he investigating another aspect of the functioning of language—one that bypassed conventional linguistic codes and sign relations?

We can say firmly that for Saussure himself his work on anagrams was not a critique of the sign or an indication that readers are free to produce meaning according to their own devices. Saussure assumed that anagrams were governed by strict supplementary conventions; discovering them was not a form of self-expression or escape from constraint. Moreover, for Saussure the anagrams, or "hypograms," as he sometimes called them, did not reveal a secret, subversive meaning but provided other words (in fact, proper names) that emphasized what the text was already discussing: "the hypogram is very much concerned with emphasizing a name, a word, making a point of repeating its syllables, and in this way giving it a second, contrived being, added, as it were, to the original of the word."[10] Anagrams reinforce the meaning

[8]Ibid., p. 99.
[9]Ibid., pp. 105–6.
[10]Ibid., p. 18.

carried by other signs of the text rather than undercutting that meaning.

What can we say of Saussure's theory? One might place it in a psychoanalytic perspective and say that he discovered a particular case of what can be called the "insistence of the letter in the unconscious." In reading over something one has written, it is quite a familiar experience to discover that one has, without meaning to, repeated a word in two different senses or used similar-sounding words in close proximity; the explanation presumably is that a key word has lingered in the subconscious and helped to determine the choice of subsequent words. Psychoanalytic evidence, especially the examples in Freud's *Psychopathology of Everyday Life* (1914), suggests the importance of purely verbal connections, connections of a punning and anagrammatic sort, in the workings of the unconscious. Thus one would have every reason to expect that poetic language, which is not governed by specific communicative ends and which gives greater scope to associative processes, would involve a certain amount of anagrammatic repetition, even if the poet were not intentionally seeking it.

If, as Saussure believed, the convincing cases of anagrams involve repetition of words already in the text, then one can relate anagrams to other poetic processes. In Baudelaire's phrase "Je sent*is* ma gorge serrée par la main *terri*ble de l'hystérie," the italicized sounds *i s terri* reproduce exactly the final word, *hystérie*. Presumably the poet wanted a rich echoing sound texture and happened to create an anagram. Consider this stanza from a sonnet by Gerard Manley Hopkins:

As kingfishers catch fire, dragonflies draw flame;
As tumbled over rim in roundy wells
Stones ring; like each tucked string tells, each hung bell's
Bow swung finds tongue to fling out broad its name.

We could find dispersed here the sounds of *flame* (line 4, *fling*
. . . n*ame*), C*hrist* (*k, r,* and *i* in line 1; *st* twice in line 3), and
many other words, but these potential anagrams seem less
important than the echoes of "*king-fi*shers *c*atch *fi*re" and
"h*ung* . . . sw*ung* . . . to*ngue*," which suggest that creatures
and objects fling out their names in what they do. Anagrammatic repetition is related to rhyme, alliteration, assonance—
patterns that form on the phonemic level through repetition
of the constituents of signs rather than signs themselves.
Saussure himself, who attended to repetition of various sorts
in his work on anagrams, noted:

> It is as easy to suppose that, if one had begun with the
> ANAGRAM, the repetition of syllables issuing from it
> would have produced the idea of an order to be created
> from phoneme to phoneme, an alliteration leading to a
> balance of sounds, as to suppose the opposite, namely
> that poets were first attentive to the balance of sounds
> and then found it natural, given that the same sounds
> had to be repeated, to choose those which alluded at the
> same time to a name of which everyone would have been
> aware.[11]

Either way, anagrams are related to a practice of repetition,
and whether complete anagrams form may not, finally, be
crucial, though this lends a neatness to repetition and recu-
perates it as an identifiable sign.

Anagrams then would be a special case of a more general
phenomenon, whose importance in the functioning of language would need to be assessed. In Saussure's account of
language as a system of signs, a language consists of signs
which are the product of contrasts between elements that
themselves do not carry meaning but have only a differential

[11]Ibid., p. 95.

function. As we saw in Chapter 2, these basic units are entirely defined by their ability to differentiate higher-level units, signs; the phoneme /b/ is the intersection of the contrasts that differentiate *bat* from *pat, cat, fat, gat, hat, rat, sat, tat, vat,* or *bet* from *jet, let, met, pet, net, set, debt, vet.* If, when looking at a text, one begins to attend not to signs but to other patterns formed by their constituents—letters or phonemes—then a different perspective opens: the possibility of other signifying processes working beneath or alongside the manifest signs of the text.

Saussure himself was inclined to consider the repetition of letters important only when they could be seen as a dispersal or concealment of regular signs relevant to the text's explicit statement. He thus insured, while identifying another level and mechanism of signification, that its textual energies passed through ordinary signs: anagrammatic repetition signified by forming proper names. The idea of looking at the constituents of signs for their role in anagrams establishes, though, two possibilities: (1) finding anagrams and other traces of signs that do not explicitly appear in the text and that might carry a counter-message, and (2) finding patterns of repetition that are not easily resolvable into regular signs—as in "kingfishers catch fire," "proud as a peacock," or "I like Ike." Once one begins to think of letters as possible constituents of other patterns, one is approaching language in a new way.

From this perspective, language seems not so much a system of signs, each joining a signifier with its signified, as an infinite pattern of echoes and repetitions, where readers are confronted with the problem of determining which of numerous possible patterns to pursue, which to endow with significance. (Saussure looked for anagrams of relevant proper names, but he might instead have looked for irrelevant ones, or for vowel patterns or consonant clusters.) Signs are not simply given to perception: to perceive the signifier at all is to confer on some patterns and not on others the status of meaningful expressions. On the one hand, then, meaning seems to be produced by the reader, who pursues some leads and not others; but on the other hand, linguistic effects of various sorts may be produced by forces that do not seem to involve linguistic conventions at all, as in the sound patterning of advertising slogans or of poetry, which may do its work without a reader or listener explicitly becoming aware of it. Either way, the model of language as a system of signs seems under attack. The idea that prior linguistic conventions enable listeners or readers to identify signifiers and know their meaning seems to be undermined from both sides by the processes anagrams expose: there is patterning that seems to work without prior conventions or listeners' recognition, and there is patterning that seems willfully created by readers, who must determine what to count as a signifier.

This vision of language, which one glimpses as one struggles with Saussure to perceive key names and other patterns that seem to be anagrammatically dispersed in the text, has been of special interest as a critique of the views of language implied in what is called the "logocentrism" of the Western tradition. We generally think of language as a mediating system through which thought is expressed or physically manifested. The ideal would be to contemplate thought directly, without the intervention of signs, but we must have recourse to signs, in which material signifiers stand for or represent spiritual signifieds. Signifiers are external appearances that should be as transparent as possible and give access to concepts themselves, or to what the speaker, in that revealing English phrase, "has in mind."

From even this brief description one can draw many elements of logocentrism, the familiar conceptual framework of Western thought: ordinary ideas about language rely on hierarchical oppositions between reality and appearance, between essence and accident, between inside and outside, between meaning and form, where the first term takes priority and the second is conceived in relation to it, as derivative and dependent. The general pattern here opposes a reality, a foundation—an order of truth, logic, reason, in short the *logos* (whence the term "logocentrism")—to appearances, accidents, contingencies, representations. Thus, signifiers are conceived as standing for or providing access to concepts, which are in principle independent of their means of manifestation or expression. The thought should not be confused with or affected by its means of expression. The scandal of the pun, for example, is that it treats a supposedly accidental and contingent relationship between signifiers (say *history* and *his story* or *write* and *right*) as if it were a conceptual relationship. If such confusions persisted, they might disrupt the hierarchical opposition and threaten the autonomy and priority of meaning/truth/essence/inside by allowing it to be affected by form/appearance/accident/outside.

An aspect of logocentrism particularly relevant to language has been the notion that sounds represent meanings which are present in the consciousness of the speaker—what the speaker has in mind. Now Saussure has a complicated relationship to logocentrism, as will emerge yet further in the next section, when we discuss Jacques Derrida's reading of the *Course*, but on this point we can say that Saussure's resistance to logocentrism does not stem from or require an interest in anagrams. The signifier is not an expression of an autonomous concept or mental presence first because language is not a nomenclature and second because what might be present to consciousness is a network of differences. If, as Saussure writes, the most precise characteristic of every sign is to be what others are not, and a signified consists of traces of what contrasts with it, then one cannot speak of the presence to consciousness of a single autonomous signified. When I utter the word *green*, such "concept" as might be present is perhaps best represented as the combination of "not-blue," "not-red," "not-yellow," etc.—a bundle of nots. The meaning of *green* is a space in an interpersonal network of differences. To *give* the meaning is not to recover something that was present when I uttered the word but to fill up the space with other signs, to characterize some of the distinctions that define it.

Saussure's insistence on the differential nature of linguistic units works against logocentrism, but the picture of language tantalizingly offered by the pursuit of anagrams seems to go further, questioning the idea that language is a system of signs by suggesting (1) that there are forces at work below the level of the sign, and (2) that signs are not phenomenally given, so that the decision to treat certain patterns and not others as signifying patterns is an imposition of meaning, not a recognition of conventionally established signs. The concept of the sign, based on the distinction between form and meaning or the sensible and the intelligible, certainly belongs to the logocentrism of Western thought, so that if Saussure's work on anagrams provides a glimpse of forces in language that disrupt the economy of the sign, it identifies what logocentrism works to repress or set aside as irrelevant to the nature of language.

There are two lessons to be drawn from the example of anagrams, but they are lessons that might come more easily from a text such as Joyce's *Finnegans Wake*, which of course was not available to Saussure. *Finnegans Wake* seems woven of terms that resemble signs of various languages but sometimes do not coincide with them:

And stand up tall! Straight. I want to see you looking fine for me. With your brandnew big green belt and all. Blooming in the very lotust and second to nill, Budd! When you're in the buckly shuit Rosensharonals near did for you. Fiftyseven and three, cosh, with the bulge.

Proudpurse Alby with his pooraroon Eireen, they'll.
Pride, comfytousness, enevy![12]

Knowledge of context provides various plots—for instance,
a wife and mother asking a husband to show off his new
clothes, or his sexual potency—but interpretation is above
all an exploration of relations between the forms presented
by the text and signs of various languages: *shuit* suggests, of
course, *shit*, but perhaps more pertinently *shirt, suit,* or *shoes*
(because of the *buckle* in *buckly,* though *buckly suit* suggests
"birthday suit"). *Rosensharonals* looks like a proper name (a
tailor?) but evokes "Rose of Sharon," which goes with
"bloom," "lotus," and "budd." *Budd* itself is a term of ad-
dress ("Hey, Bud!") or the Gaelic for "penis" (which goes
with "Stand up tall"), and "nill, Budd!" contains an anagram
of "Dublin"—Dublin spelled backward—which figures
prominently in the *Wake,* and here is evoked with its "green
belt and all," prior to the political scenario of "Proudpurse
Alby" (perfidious Albion?) and his "pooraroon Eireen"
("poor Eire" but also "Eileen Aroon," which means "Eileen,
my darling").

Here, as in the case of anagrams, readers feel on the one
hand compelled to choose what to pursue, what to treat as
significant, yet, on the other hand, subjected to a process of
repetition, in which signs echo other signs, perhaps in languages they do not know. Readers feel both that there is
meaning insistent in the text (in the words' relations to other
words) and that one must creatively produce meaning by
pursuing some connections, associating forms in the text with
particular signs.

The two lessons, then, are, first, that the words of a work

[12]James Joyce, *Finnegans Wake* (London: Faber, 1939), p. 620. I am indebted to Derek Attridge's discussion of this passage in "Unpacking the
Portmanteau," forthcoming in *The Call of the Phoneme,* ed. J. Culler.

are rooted in other antecedent words, whose traces they bear in different ways: anagrammatically, perhaps, but also by echoes of various kinds. Though this is made obvious by portmanteau words ("comfytousness" "famillionarily") that explicitly allude to others, or by unintelligible sequences that need to be interpreted as transformations of other words ("shuit," "buckly"), it is true of all linguistic sequences, which are composed of syllables from other sequences and refer obliquely to these sequences by their similarities and differences. Language is a network of traces, with signifiers spilling over into one another. One cannot, then, say with confidence what is in the text and what is outside it—a generalizable lesson from the case of anagrams. One must follow the forces of attraction that link signifiers in the most productive ways.

But second, these examples show that to interpret any features of a text at all is to recuperate them as signs. To perceive something as a signifier, to make it signify, is to correlate it with a signified, albeit an empty one. Happy talk about the play of signifiers must reckon with the fact that there can be no signifiers without signifieds. Saussure recognized anagrammatic sequences and treated them as signifiers when they spelled words whose meaning he knew, and in working to read *Finnegans Wake* we treat forms as significant by relating them to known signs that enable us to posit either alternative signifieds (*shuit* is "suit" or "shoes"), or composite signifieds (*shuit* is "shirt, suit, and shoes together"), or metalinguistic signifieds (*shuit* signifies "the artificiality of ordinary distinctions"). The most radical play of the signifier still requires and works through the positing of signifieds.

It may well be that what we are repeatedly confronting in these examples is the phenomenon of change in semiotic systems, the way in which new meanings can be produced and codes or conventions modified or extended. We frequently encounter situations in which language or a configuration of other symbolic material promises meaning but resists it: promises meaning, in that we are willing to grant it a signifying status because of its resemblance to recognized signifiers or because of the pattern it seems to belong to, but resists in that we cannot tell which convention is relevant (which of various possible signs it is) or in what way we should modify a convention to deal with it. The most interesting semiotic objects are those which insistently intimate their relation to sign systems but are hard to place and resist easy interpretation. They don't quite fit the system's categories; they seem to escape it, to violate what one takes to be its rules. But since we are governed by the semiological imperative, *Try to make sense of things*, we struggle with the refractory or evasive object, straining and extending our notions of significance, modifying and extrapolating from the rules of our system, or bringing two codes into juxtaposition to set off an interpretive interplay. We encounter here a point made earlier about literature: if an explicit semiotic code provided interpretations for literary works, literature would have little interest, and authors, if they wrote at all, would strive to violate this code.

Semiotics treats meaning as a product of a system of conventions, and this model fits much of our lives, where a red octagonal sign means "stop," a particular uniform denotes police, and *Apportez-moi le livre rouge* means "Bring me the red book." But the most engaging and often frustrating situations are those where we have trouble fitting codes to phenomena and where meaning as the product of conventions seems to be supplanted by a tension between two other notions of meaning: meaning as a property of texts or objects, and meaning as significance I can attribute to objects. Neither conception on its own is very defensible, but the situation where we struggle to discover a meaning that resides in the object and at the same time feel that we must invent or produce a meaning seems exemplary for semiotics. We are attracted to such moments or situations, which seem to place us on the borders of codes and conventions, where codes are tested, perhaps transformed, and meaning must be produced. The interest Saussure's work on anagrams has provoked comes in part from its practical dramatization of the tension between finding and positing meaning, a tension that lies before and behind the conventions of semiotic systems.

Rereading Saussure

Michel Foucault makes a useful distinction between founders of disciplines and what he calls founders of discursive practices. The founder of a discursive practice—an activity of discourse and commentary—is someone like Marx or Freud who establishes a domain of discourse in which advances take the form of reinterpretations of the original text: Marxism progresses by reinterpretations of Marx, just as psychoanalysis is driven by rereadings of Freud. Founders of disciplines may have a revolutionary historical importance, but advances in their disciplines do not take the form of reinterpretations of founding texts: physicists do not do physics by writing about Newton. So far we have considered Saussure as a founder of the modern discipline of linguistics, a discipline which, as one might predict, generally proceeds with its debates without referring to Saussure. We have also treated him as a founder of the potential discipline of semiotics. But Saussure has played the other role as well; his *Course in General Linguistics* is one of the basic texts of the discursive realm today known by the nickname "theory," and discussions of signification in various fields have taken the form of revisions or reinterpretations of Saussure. Three areas in which important rereadings of Saussure have occurred are Marxism, psychoanalysis, and deconstruction.

134

Marxism

Attempts in Marxist theory to correct crude economic determinism, which relegates cultural activity to a derivative superstructure, must find ways of dealing with language and symbolic activity generally. This task can be conceived as an attempt to correct the "idealist presuppositions" in Saussurian sign theory. In *Language and Materialism*, Rosalind Coward and John Ellis note that the Saussurian treatment of language as a sign system and the extension of this perspective to social practices conceived as languages can, if reread from a materialist angle, help to cure a "central failing in Marxist thought and practice." "Because all the practices that make up the social totality take place in language, it becomes possible to consider language as the place in which the social individual is constructed" and to undertake "for the first time, a scientific analysis of the concept of the 'human,' which we suggest is a fundamental presupposition of bourgeois ideology."[13]

Coward and Ellis take Saussure's key contribution to be the separating of signifier and signified so as to study the relations among signifiers in the production of meaning. Saussure's claim that meaning is the product of differences "had a more radical potentiality, since the signifier could be seen to have an active function in creating and determining the signified."[14] The prospect that meaning in general, and with it crucial features of the social order, might be produced rather than given, and that there are processes of production to study, has been important for a number of Marxist theorists who are willing to grant a relative autonomy to the semiotic realm in which subjects and ideology are produced.

Saussure's account of the sign has also been reinterpreted

[13] *Language and Materialism* (London: Routledge, 1977), p. 2.
[14] Ibid., p. 3.

in a more specific way in Marxist discussions of value, particularly those of Jean Baudrillard, who, perhaps inspired by Saussure's own use of economic metaphors in the *Course*, identifies the structure of the sign with the structure of the commodity. Marx distinguished the use-value of a commodity (its true usefulness to an individual) from its exchange-value (its value in the economic system of exchange), and he regarded the latter as an appearance which had no systematic relation to its use-value. This structure, associated with "commodity-fetishism," is that of the sign: exchange-value is a signifier and use-value a signified. Baudrillard argues that no natural relation connects or should connect the two, any more than it does the signifier and signified. But against Marxism that takes use-value as given, as the true meaning of a commodity, from which its signifier in capitalistic systems unfortunately differs, Baudrillard argues that this use-value must be understood as a signified that only appears to have an existence apart from its signifier (exchange-value); this signified is in fact produced by the signifying system to provide a ground or alibi for the signifier, as the value it supposedly represents. Asserting that the commodity is the sign and the sign is the commodity, Baudrillard uses the revised Saussurian model to contest Marxist accounts which locate semiotic activity in a superstructural realm (ideology) that reflects a narrowly defined economic realm and to maintain that "ideology is actually that very form that traverses both the production of signs and material production."[15]

What seems crucial in Saussure for contemporary Marxism is the suggestion that signifiers do not simply represent signifieds but articulate and thus, in a sense, produce them. This skewing of Saussurian symmetry makes it possible to imagine a materialist account of a productive process,

[15]*Pour une critique de l'économie politique du signe* (Paris: Gallimard, 1972), p. 173.

integrating the semiotic and the economic in a single conceptual framework.

Psychoanalysis

The most powerful theorist of contemporary psychoanalysis, Jacques Lacan, presents his work as a return to Freud in the light of Saussure, though this also involves a reinterpretation and modification of Saussure, so that his remarks on language will apply to the production of the subject in the symbolic order. If, as Saussure argued, language is not a nomenclature that expresses pre-existing meaning but a structure of differential signifiers and signifieds, which contrast and combine with one another to produce effects of meaning, then it can be identified with the systems of symbolic relations and positions that produce subjects. "Through the word," Lacan writes, "—already a presence made of absence—... there is born the world of meaning of a particular language in which the world of things will come to be arranged. Through that which comes to be embodied only by being the trace of a nothingness and whose support cannot thereafter be impaired, the concept . . . engenders the thing. . . . It is the world of words creates the world of things. . . . Man speaks, then, but it is because the symbol has made him man."[16]

Not only does language suffuse the symbolic order, which produces a social world and subjects positioned in it; by Lacan's most famous dictum, "the unconscious is structured like a language." The operations of condensation and displacement, which for Freud characterized unconscious processes, are associated with the operations of substitution and combination instantiated by the two axes of language. More

[16]*Ecrits: A Selection* (London: Tavistock, 1977), p. 65. For discussion, see Kaja Silverman, *The Subject of Semiotics* (New York: Oxford University Press, 1983).

generally, "if what Freud discovered and rediscovers with a perpetually increasing sense of shock has any meaning, it is that the displacement of the signifier determines the subjects in their acts, in their destiny, in their refusals, in their blindnesses, in their end and in their fate, their innate gifts and social acquisitions notwithstanding, without regard for character or sex, and that, willingly or not, everything that might be considered the stuff of psychology, kit and caboodle, will follow the path of the signifier."[17]

As this passage suggests, Saussure's distinction between signifier and signified is crucial for Lacan, who calls the Saussurian model of the sign an indispensable algorithm: "S/s, which is read as the signifier over the signified, 'over' corresponding to the bar separating the two stages."[18] Distinguishing signified from signifier is what made possible "an exact study of the connections proper to the signifier and of the extent of their function in the genesis of the signified"— that is, the way in which signifiers derive their meaning from the play of contrasts and combinations. But where Saussure saw signifier and signified as arbitrarily but indissolubly joined, like the two sides of a sheet of paper, Lacan takes the bar of the diagram as indication of a crucial separation: the play of signifiers promises meaning without necessarily delivering; there is, as Lacan calls it, a sliding of the signified under the signifier. His antipathy to anything that might be said to be *the* meaning of a sign emerges particularly in passages where, describing "the fundamental distinction between signifier and signified" and the two networks of relations that they organize, he associates the signifier with the linguistic system and the signified with utterances:

The first structure, that of the signifier, is the synchronic structure of language material insofar as in that structure

[17]Lacan, "Seminar on 'The Purloined Letter,'" *Yale French Studies* 48 (1972), 60.
[18]*Ecrits*, p. 149.

each element assumes its precise function by being different from the others; this is the principle of distribution that alone governs the function of the elements of the language at its different levels. . . .

The second network, that of the signified, is the diachronic set of the concretely pronounced discourses, which reacts historically on the first, just as the structure of the first governs the pathways of the second. The dominant factor here is the unity of signification, which proves never to be resolved into a pure indication of the real but always refers back to another signification.[19]

Here Lacan dubiously relegates signification to the temporal unfolding of discourse, which he calls the network of the signified. It would prove difficult to analyze the synchronic structure of language as a system without referring to signifieds, for it is difference of meaning that enables one to identify different signifiers. But Lacan's reinterpretation of Saussure is faithful to the mechanisms encountered in the investigation of anagrams, where one continually encounters repetition of what are offered as signifiers without any confident identification of signifieds. Reinterpreting Saussure as a theoretician of the signifier enables Lacan to uncover the most radical insights of Freud's writings, which become exemplary investigations and instantiations of the signifying forces at work in minds and texts.

Deconstruction

Deconstruction is Jacques Derrida's term for a critique that demonstrates how the hierarchical oppositions of Western thought are undone, subverted, or "deconstructed," exposed as constructions or ideological impositions, by writings that affirm and rely on them. Derrida's analyses undertake a cri-

[19]Ibid., p. 126.

tique of the logocentrism of Western thought, which, as we saw earlier, can be characterized as the postulation of an order of meaning (thought, truth, reason, logic, the Word, the *logos*) conceived as foundation: prior to and independent of signs, appearances, etc., in which it may be manifested. A major instance of logocentrism has been the phonocentrism of theories of language: the treatment of writing as the representation of a representation, an artificial substitute for speech, and the attempt to conceive of language in general on the model of speech. Derrida argues that to set writing aside as derivative and parasitic is a way of ignoring certain features of language or aspects of its functioning. If writing, which seems inescapably to involve impersonality, distance, the need for interpretation, and the possibility of misunderstanding, is treated as a mere technical device, secondary and derivative, irrelevant to the nature of language itself, then one can take as the essence of language an ideal associated with speech: in particular, the experience of hearing oneself speak, where hearing and understanding seem to be inseparable, where signifier and signified seem immediately joined in a sign, where the expression seems bound to the meaning it arises to express.

One deconstructs the hierarchical opposition of speech and writing by showing that the qualities attributed to writing in the attempt to demote it or set it aside apply to speech as well. Here, for Derrida, a reading of Saussure plays a crucial role, providing classic assertions of logocentric positions but offering also instances of principles that undo or subvert them, exposing them as constructions or impositions. Derrida's *Of Grammatology*, which disrupts the hierarchical opposition between speech and writing by speculating on the possibility of approaching language through a science of writing, undertakes a reading of passages in the *Course* where Saussure treats writing as a deformation of speech. Although he does specifically exclude sound from the linguistic system and insists on the formal character of linguistic units, Saussure nevertheless maintains that "the object of linguistic analysis is not defined by the combination of the spoken and the written word; the spoken word alone constitutes the object" (*Course*, 23–24; *Cours*, 45). He denounces the "dangers" of writing, which "disguises" language and even on occasion "usurps" the role of speech. "The tyranny of writing" is powerful and insidious, leading, for example, to errors of pronunciation that are "pathological," a corruption or infection of the natural spoken forms. Linguists who attend to written forms are "falling into the trap." The moral fervor that marks Saussure's discussion indicates that something important is at stake when writing, supposedly a representation of speech, threatens the purity of the system it serves.

But if writing can affect speech, then the relationship is more complicated than first appeared. The hierarchical scheme that treats writing as derivative and dependent is further skewed by Saussure's recourse to the example of writing to explain linguistic units. How can one illustrate the notion of a purely differential unit? "Since an identical state of affairs is observable in writing, another system of signs, we shall use writing to draw some comparisons that will clarify the whole issue" (*Course*, 119; *Cours*, 165). The letter *t*, for example, can be written in various ways so long as it remains distinct from *l, f, i, d,* etc. There are no essential features that must be preserved; its identity is purely relational.

Thus writing, which Saussure claimed ought not to be the object of linguistic inquiry, turns out to be the best illustration of the nature of linguistic units. Speech is to be understood as a form of writing, an instance of the basic linguistic mechanism manifested in writing. Saussure's text brings about this reversal: the announced hierarchy that makes writing a derivative form of speech, a parasitic mode of representation added to speech, is inverted and speech is presented, explained, as a form of writing. This gives us a new concept of writing: a generalized writing that would have as subspecies a vocal writing and a graphic writing.

The possibility of treating speech as a special case of a generalized writing is a consequence of Saussure's discovery of the purely differential identity of linguistic units. The more rigorously he pursues his investigation, the more he is led to insist on the purely relational nature of the linguistic system: "in the linguistic system there are only differences, without positive terms" (*Course,* 120; *Cours,* 166). Therefore sound itself cannot belong to the system: it is a medium in which elements may be manifested, like black ink, or the marble of monuments. As Derrida explains, the principle that language is a system of differences generates a powerful critique of logocentrism, undermining the attempt to found a theory of language on positive entities which might be taken as given. If in the linguistic system there are only differences,

the play of differences involves syntheses and referrals that prevent there from being at any moment or in any way a simple element that is present in and of itself and refers only to itself. Whether in written or spoken discourse, no element can function as a sign without relating to another element which is not simply present. This linkage means that each "element"—phoneme or grapheme—is constituted with reference to the trace in it of the other elements of the sequence or system. This linkage, this weaving, is the *text,* which is produced only through the transformation of another text. Nothing, either in the elements or in the system, is anywhere simply present or absent. There are only, everywhere, differences and traces of traces.[20]

[20]*Positions* (Chicago: University of Chicago Press, 1981), p. 26. For discussion of deconstruction, see my *On Deconstruction* (Ithaca: Cornell University Press, 1982).

This line of argument leads, among other things, to a critique of Saussure's notion of the sign, with its firm distinction between signifier and signified. Since the signifier is not itself material but a purely differential or relational entity, the difference between signifier and signified is not one of substance—the one material, the other spiritual, or the one sensible, the other intelligible. The difference is purely functional: the signifier is whatever promises signification, but a signified can play the role of signifier in its turn, as we discover when we look a word up in a dictionary to discover its meaning and find, of course, another word, which we can also look up. Saussure's concept of the sign, which is presented as based on the distinction between the sensible and the intelligible, belongs to logocentrism, but he also provides the instruments for its deconstruction. Derrida explains:

Maintenance of the rigorous distinction—an essential and juridical distinction—between the *signans* [signifier] and the *signatum* [signified] and the equation between the *signatum* and the concept leaves open in principle the possibility of conceiving of a *signified concept in itself*, a concept simply present to thought, independent from the linguistic system, that is to say from a system of signifiers. In leaving this possibility open, and it is so left by the very principle of the opposition between signifier and signified and thus of the sign, Saussure contradicts the critical acquisition of which we have spoken. He accedes to the traditional demand for what I have proposed to call a "transcendental signified," which in itself or in its essence would not refer to any signifier, which would transcend the chain of signs and at a certain moment would no longer itself function as signifier. On the contrary, though, from the moment one puts in question the possibility of such a transcendental signified and recognizes that every signified is also in the position

of signifier, the distinction between signifier and signified and thus the notion of sign becomes problematic at
its root.[21]

This does not, of course, mean that the notion of the sign
could or should be scrapped; on the contrary, the distinction
between what signifies and what is signified, however problematic, seems essential to any thought whatever, certainly to
Saussure's linguistic project. What this argument suggests,
above all, is the necessity of regarding the distinction of signifier and signified as functional and provisional rather than
substantial, so that any signified may be seen as a signifier in
turn. By showing that Saussure's own text provides a critique
of the concept of the sign it employs, Derrida uses it to illumi-
nate the most intractable problems of signification. The
power and pertinence of a text like Saussure's may depend
upon the resourcefulness with which it puts in question the
hierarchical oppositions on which it necessarily relies.

A further point of interest in Derrida's rereading of Saussure—another moment where Saussure's explicit argument
relies on hierarchical oppositions that some of his principles
teach one to question—is the procedure by which Saussure
establishes his doctrine of the arbitrary nature of the sign.
"Onomatopoeic words," Saussure writes,

> might be held to show that a choice of signifier is not al-
> ways arbitrary. But such words are never organic ele-
> ments of a linguistic system. Moreover, they are far
> fewer than is generally believed. Words such as *fouet*
> ["whip"] or *glas* ["knell"] may strike some ears as hav-
> ing a certain suggestive sonority. But to see that this is in
> no way intrinsic to the words themselves, it suffices to
> look at their Latin origins. *Fouet* comes from Latin *fagus*

[21]*Positions*, pp. 19–20.

("beech tree") and *glas* from Latin *classicum* ("trumpet call"). The suggestive quality of the modern pronunciation of these words is a fortuitous result of phonetic evolution. (*Course*, 69; *Cours*, 101–2)

As Derrida notes in *Glas*, a formidable book whose title comes in part from this passage, the recourse to etymology in discussing the "intrinsic" character of a particular sign is strange in a theorist who imperiously distinguishes between synchronic facts and diachronic facts, but odder still is the exclusion of "fortuitous" by one who tells us that language is essentially fortuitous. In order to define the linguistic sign as *essentially* fortuitous—arbitrary—Saussure excludes fortuitous *motivation.*

These paradoxical moves, like the exclusion of writing, alert us to the possibility that what is being set aside in order to leave a pure linguistic sign or linguistic system may in fact be a significant aspect of language: fortuitous motivation might be a general mechanism of language. Even if one grants Saussure's argument that onomatopoeias are never pure, never solidly grounded in resemblance, one might nevertheless take an interest in the contamination of arbitrariness by motivation, whether this motivation is produced by the craftsmanship of poets, by the fortuitous effects of linguistic evolution, by the keen eye of readers looking for anagrams, by the errors of speakers, or by the mechanisms of the unconscious. One might wish to maintain, with Saussure, that in a sense the structure of French or English is not affected by the potential suggestiveness of various signifiers, but one could also wonder, with Derrida, whether the language one speaks or writes is not always exposed to the contamination of arbitrary signs by suggestions of imitative motivation, whether effects of motivation are not inseparable from the workings of language. "What if this mimesis meant that the internal system of language does not exist, or that one never uses it, or at least that one only uses it by contaminating it, and that this contamination is inevitable and thus regular and 'normal,' belongs to the system and its functioning, *en fasse partie*, that is to say, both is a part of it and also makes the system, which is the whole, part of a whole larger than itself?"[22]

The very sentence in which Saussure sets aside motivation displays an effect of motivation in a way which suggests that discourse may be driven by precisely the sort of phenomena he wishes to exclude from language. "*Fouet* and *glas*," he writes, "may *strike* [*peuvent frapper*] some ears as having a certain suggestive sonority." *Fouet* and *glas* both strike the ear, perhaps, because whips and bells strike: the term for what words do as they make a noise seems generated by the examples, or the choice of examples is generated by what words are said to do to the ear. This sentence, working to remotivate and thus link together supposedly arbitrary signs, displays a principle by which discourse frequently operates and suggests that arbitrary signs of the linguistic system may be part of a larger discursive system in which effects of motivation, demotivation, and remotivation are always occurring. Relations between signifiers or between signifiers and signifieds can always produce effects, whether conscious or unconscious. This cannot be set aside as irrelevant to language, and Saussure, resourcefully read, helps to put us on its track.

Rereading Saussure, in the analytical enterprise of deconstruction, as in Marxism and psychoanalysis, alerts us to problems of discourse and complexities of signification that suffuse the practices of a culture and require semiotic analysis. All three analytical projects seem especially interested in exploiting the suggestion that meaning is produced, not given, and that the play of differences of the signifier shape signifieds. The attempt to show, in each area, that meanings or truths we might be inclined to take as given are the prod-

---

[22]Derrida, *Glas* (Paris: Galilée, 1974), p. 109.

uct of semiotic systems has been a powerful means of demystification and analysis.

Conclusions

"In the whole history of science," wrote the philosopher Ernst Cassirer, "there is perhaps no more fascinating chapter than the rise of the 'new science' of linguistics. In its importance it may very well be compared to the new science of Galileo which, in the seventeenth century, changed our whole concept of the physical world."[23] I have tried to outline Ferdinand de Saussure's role in the rise of modern linguistics and suggest why this is a fascinating episode in recent intellectual history. But Cassirer's bold comparison of modern linguistics with the new science of Galileo is more difficult to evaluate. What does it mean and how could it be substantiated?

For Cassirer, the crucial and revolutionary aspect of modern linguistics is Saussure's insistence on the primacy of relations and systems of relations. Here, in its fundamental concepts and methodological premises, Saussure's theory of language is an exceptionally clear expression of the formal strategies by which a whole series of disciplines, from physics to painting, transformed themselves in the late nineteenth and early twentieth centuries and became modern.

The strategy can be stated most simply as a shift in focus, from objects to relations. It is relationships that create and define objects, not the other way around. The philosopher of science Alfred North Whitehead offers a general statement of the problem: "The misconception which has haunted philosophic literature throughout the centuries is the notion of 'independent existence.' There is no such mode of existence;

---

[23] "Structuralism in Modern Linguistics," *Word* 1 (1945), 99.

every entity is to be understood in terms of the way it is inter-woven with the rest of the universe." And in his book *Science and the Modern World* (1925) he shows that new discoveries in science produced so many complexities that a fundamental shift in perspective was necessary if the various disciplines were to come to terms with themselves and their objects. Physics discovered that it was exceedingly difficult to explain electricity and electromagnetic phenomena in terms of dis-crete units of matter and their movement. The solution seemed to be to reverse the problem: instead of taking matter as prime, and trying to define the laws governing its behavior, why not take energy itself, electrical energy, as prime and de-fine matter in terms of electromagnetic forces? This change in perspective leads to the discovery of new scientific objects: an electron is not a positive entity in the old sense; it is a product of a field of force, a node in a system of relations, and, like a phoneme, it does not exist independently of these relations.

What Whitehead calls the "materialism" of the nineteenth century, the empiricism which grants ontological primacy to objects, gives way, he says, to a "theory of relativity" in the broadest sense: a theory based on the primacy of relations. "On the materialist theory," Whitehead writes, "there is ma-terial which endures. On the organic theory the only endur-ances are structures of activity." Emphasis falls on the struc-tures. "The event is what it is by reason of the unification within itself of a multiplicity of relationships." Outside these systems of relations, it is nothing.

Saussure, of course, states these themes clearly, not as as-pects of some diffuse world view but as methodological pos-tulates that are necessary if language is to be properly ana-lyzed. And alongside Saussure's affirmations we may place the unequivocal statement of the painter Georges Braque: "I do not believe in things; I believe in relationships." This is, perhaps, the true Modernist credo. What is Cubism if not an assertion of the primacy of relationships? In Cubist paintings objects lose their hitherto unquestioned primacy; they emerge with difficulty from the interaction of lines and planes; the three-dimensional space which supports ordinary objects is broken down in an attempt to represent a variety of perspectives and relations simultaneously. Or again, in Modernist literature one can observe the shift by which both poetry and the novel become less directly mimetic, less concerned with the representation of recognizable objects and scenes, and more interested in effects of juxtaposition, where relational values—relations between words or among various types of discourse—become the primary constituents of the work of art.

In various fields or disciplines, shifts in technique have led to a concentration on systems of relation. This is the basis of Cassirer's bold claim: that for the thought of our century the world is no longer essentially a collection of independent entities, of autonomous objects, but a series of relational systems.

This move from object to structure is indeed a major shift in our conception of the world, but it is not clear how far the role of Galileo should fall to Saussure and Saussurian linguistics. From a historical point of view, his theory of language seems an exceptionally clear expression of a shift which was taking place simultaneously, if less explicitly, in a variety of fields; an expression or example more than a primary cause. Indeed, it seems likely that if Saussure is ever to be cast in the role of twentieth-century Galileo, his right to that position will depend on the discipline and mode of thought which he was actually instrumental in founding: semiotics. To bring us to see social life and culture in general as a series of sign systems which a linguistic model can help us to analyze—this is the contribution which might eventually make him comparable to Galileo.

But of course it is too early to judge the real significance of Saussure in the intellectual history of our century, for work in the field of semiotics has only recently begun, and it is not yet clear whether it will indeed become a dominant intellectual movement of our time. If it does become a major presence, a central discipline, this will be due to the efforts of many people besides Saussure; but his vision of a semiology that would encompass linguistics while taking it as a model has led others to give concrete expression to the semiotic perspective: we live among signs and must try not only to grasp their meaning but especially to understand the conventions responsible for their meaning. It is Saussure who stands behind the claim, which many people would today espouse, that to study human beings is essentially to study the various systems by which our cultures organize and give meaning to the world and produce human subjects.

Further Reading

Saussure's Writings

Course in General Linguistics, trans. Wade Baskin. New York: McGraw-Hill, 1966. New trans., Roy Harris. London: Duckworth, 1983.

Cours de linguistique générale, ed. Tullio de Mauro. Paris: Payot, 1973.

Cours de linguistique générale, critical ed. by Rudolf Engler. Wiesbaden: O. Harrassowitz, 1967–74. Two volumes, four fascicules.

The *Course* is essential reading, especially parts I, II, and III. Roy Harris's translation is superior to Baskin's. Tullio de Mauro's admirable edition contains very full biographical and bibliographical information, explanatory comment, and quotations from the students' notes where they provide important variants. Engler's critical edition prints all the notes from which the *Course* was constructed.

On Saussure

Aarsleff, Hans. "Taine and Saussure," in *From Locke to Saussure: Essays on the Study of Language and Intellectual History*. Minneapolis: University of Minnesota Press, 1982.

Further Reading

Avalle, D'Arco Silvio. "La sémiologie de la narrativité chez Saussure," in *Essais de la théorie du texte*, ed. Charles Bouazis. Paris: Galilée, 1973.

Benveniste, Emile. "Saussure after Half a Century," in *Problems in General Linguistics*. Miami: University of Miami Press, 1971.

Cahiers Ferdinand de Saussure. Geneva: 1941–.

Derossi, Giorgio. *Segno e struttura linguistici nel pensiero di F. de Saussure*. Udine: Del Bianco, 1965.

Derrida, Jacques. *Of Grammatology*. Baltimore: Johns Hopkins University Press, 1976.

Godel, Robert. *Les Sources manuscrites du Cours de linguistique générale de F. de Saussure*. Geneva and Paris: Droz, 1957.

Koerner, E. F. K. *Bibliographia Saussureana*. Metuchen, N.J.: Scarecrow Press, 1972.

———. *Ferdinand de Saussure: The Origin and Development of His Linguistic Thought in Western Studies of Language*. Braunschweig: Vieweg, 1973.

Starobinski, Jean. *Words upon Words: The Anagrams of Ferdinand de Saussure*. New Haven: Yale University Press, 1979.

"The Two Saussures," Vol. I, *Semiotexte* 1, no. 2 (Fall 1974). Vol. II ("Saussure's Anagrams"), *Semiotexte* 2, no. 1 (1975). A selection of these papers appears as "Les Deux Saussures," *Recherches* 16 (September 1974).

The most perceptive study of Saussure's thought is Derossi, unfortunately available only in Italian. Koerner's bibliography lists a vast number of writings on Saussure and related topics; his monograph provides a wealth of information, especially about verbal resemblances between Saussure and possible sources, but is not theoretically acute and is best avoided. Aarsleff's essay explores a major and previously unrecognized source. Starobinski publishes many extracts from Saussure's work on anagrams, and Avalle quotes and discusses his work on medieval German legends. *Cahiers Ferdinand de Saussure* is a periodical which publishes important articles on Saussure. Derrida investigates key problems in Saussure's thought. "The Two Saussures" includes excellent discussions of linguistic theory and remarks on the anagrams. Godel's interesting study of manuscript sources is largely superseded by Engler's critical edition, which publishes the sources.

Further Reading

On the History of Linguistics

Aarsleff, Hans. *From Locke to Saussure: Essays on the Study of Language and Intellectual History*. Minneapolis: University of Minnesota Press, 1982.

Foucault, Michel. *The Order of Things: An Archaeology of the Human Sciences*. New York: Pantheon, 1971.

Harris, Roy. *The Language Makers*. Ithaca: Cornell University Press, 1980.

Lepschy, Giulio C. *A Survey of Structural Linguistics*. London: Faber, 1970.

Robins, R. H. *A Short History of Linguistics*. Bloomington: Indiana University Press, 1968.

Harris's *The Language Makers* is a brilliant and irreverent discussion of the history of thinking about language and languages. Aarsleff's detailed essays provide an authoritative account of the linguistic and philosophical tradition relevant to Saussure. Foucault's discussion in chapters 4, 7, and 8 is extremely stimulating. For more sober surveys, see Lepschy for the modern period and Robins for the premodern.

Semiotics

American Journal of Semiotics. Cambridge: Schenkman, 1981–.

Barthes, Roland. *Elements of Semiology*. New York: Hill & Wang, 1968.

Blonsky, Marshall, ed. *On Signs*. Baltimore: Johns Hopkins University Press, 1985.

Culler, Jonathan. *Structuralist Poetics: Structuralism, Linguistics, and the Study of Literature*. Ithaca: Cornell University Press, 1975.

_____. *The Pursuit of Signs: Semiotics, Literature, Deconstruction*. Ithaca: Cornell University Press, 1981.

Derrida, Jacques. *Margins of Philosophy*. Chicago: University of Chicago Press, 1982.

Eco, Umberto. *Semiotics and the Philosophy of Language*. Bloomington: Indiana University Press, 1984.

Further Reading

Innis, Robert E., ed. *Semiotics: An Introductory Anthology.* Bloomington: Indiana University Press, 1985.

Scholes, Robert. *Semiotics and Interpretation.* New Haven: Yale University Press, 1982.

Semiotica. The Hague: Mouton, 1969–.

Silverman, Kaja. *The Subject of Semiotics.* New York: Oxford University Press, 1983.

Barthes is a general introduction to the field. Silverman provides a more detailed discussion, focusing on literary theory and psychoanalysis. Of the two anthologies, Innes provides basic selections and Blonsky more adventurous writings about signs. The *American Journal of Semiotics* and *Semiotica* illustrate the range of semiotic investigation. Culler and Scholes concentrate on literature. Several articles in Derrida's book are devoted to philosophical problems of semiotics.

Index

155

Index

explanation: in modern linguistics, 15–16, 56, 88–91; in pre-Saussurian linguistics, 68–70, 77; in the social sciences, 87–91

food, semiotic approach to, 120
Foucault, Michel, 74, 93, 134
Freud, Sigmund, 15, 21, 85–91, 93, 125, 134, 137–39

Galileo, 147, 149
Gardiner, Sir Alan, 95
Geneva, University of, 17, 22
Grimm, Jacob, 74–75

Harris, Roy, 84n
Hegel, G. F. W., 86
Hittite, 80
Hjelmslev, Louis, 95–97
Hockett, Charles, 100
Hopkins, G. M., 125–26
Hume, David, 85

icon, 112–13
identity, of linguistic units, 36–39, 42–43, 46–50, 57–59, 61–62, 92, 141–42
index, 112–15
Indo-European, 22–23, 72–75, 79–80
inflectional patterns, 72–75, 77

Jakobson, Roman, 95, 97, 102
Jones, Daniel, 97
Joyce, James, 130–32
Junggrammatiker. See Neogrammarians

Lacan, Jacques, 137–39
Lamarckism, 77
language: analysis of, 41, 43–44, 51, 57–64; complexity of, 27–31, 41, 95–101; historical nature of, 45–47; as social fact, 62–64; as system, 28, 32–45, 57–62, 77, 96–97; and mind, 66–73, 102
langue, 57–64, 84, 91; and *parole,* 39–45, 52–53, 95–99, 110, 119
laryngeals, 80
legends, Saussure's work on, 121–22
Leipzig, University of, 21–22, 78
Lepschy, Giulio, 95
Lévi-Strauss, Claude, 109–10
Leviticus, abominations of, 120

linguistics: in seventeenth and eighteenth centuries, 66–72; in nineteenth century, 70–84; in twentieth century, 94–104; as model for semiotics, 107–11, 119–20
literature, 116–17, 120–27, 130–33; anagrams in, 123–28, 132
Locke, John, 67–68
logocentrism, 128–30, 140–44
Lucretius, 123
Lyons, John, 99n

Martinet, André, 95
Marx, Karl, 134–36
medicine, semiotic approach to, 113, 115
Mémoire sur le système primitif des voyelles dans les langues indoeuropéennes (Saussure), 21–22, 78–80
modernism, 16–17, 147–49
morpheme, 60–62
morphology, 60–62, 103
motivation, of signs, 29–30, 145–46
Mounin, Georges, 116n

Neogrammarians, 22, 78–82
nomenclature, 31–33, 137

onomatopoeia, 29, 144–46
Osthoff, Herman, 78

paradigmatic. *See* relations
parole. See langue
performance, linguistic, 98–99
phoneme, 60–61, 92, 96, 127
phonetics, 41–42, 53–55, 96–97
phonocentrism, 140–41
phonology, 41–42, 96–97, 102; and distinctive features, 61, 97, 102; and semiotics, 109–11
physics, 134, 148
Pictet, Adolphe, 21
Port-Royal, grammar of, 67
Prague School (of linguistics), 94, 97, 101
psychoanalysis, 125, 137–39
pun, 129

Rask, Rasmus, 74
recursive rules, 99
Reid, Wallis, 99n, 104n

Library of Congress Cataloging-in-Publication Data

Culler, Jonathan D.
    Ferdinand de Saussure.

    Bibliography: p.
    Includes index.
    1. Saussure, Ferdinand de, 1857–1913. 2. Structural linguistics. 3. Semi-
otics. I. Title.
P85.S18C8   1986   410'.92'4   86-6302
ISBN 0-8014-1917-4
ISBN 0-8014-9389-7 (pbk.)